# The Seven I AMs of Jesus

( HOW JESUS MEETS YOUR DEEPEST NEEDS )

## Phil & Linda Sommerville

faithALIVE365
Living God's Best Every Day

*The Seven I AMs of Jesus: How Jesus Meets Your Deepest Needs*

Published by Faith Alive 365

Copyright © 2012 by Phil and Linda Sommerville

ISBN 978-0-9815531-2-2

Second printing January, 2013

Cover Design by Dave Eaton Creative

Printed in the United States of America

Faith Alive 365
5958 Tanus Circle
Rocklin, CA 95677

## Praise for *The Seven I AMs of Jesus* All-Church Series

*"The 7 I AMs of Jesus All-Church Series* was an incredible Biblical adventure in the gospel of John. Over this 50 day series we saw over 60 decisions for Christ and 25 baptisms! I highly recommend this powerful series to any church." - Chuck Wysong, Lead Pastor of Bayside West Community Church, Roseville, CA

"We had some really amazing things happen during the series. People came to faith who we'd been working with for quite some time. Record numbers joined small groups. People LOVED the book. We had long time believers reenergized in their faith. We had our largest community service event ever. HUGE thanks to you for this excellent series." - Randy Sherwood, Lead Pastor of Bayside Church of Plumas Lake, CA

## Praise for *The Seven I AMs of Jesus* Book & Small Group Studies

"This 50-day devotional weaves powerful testimonies of transformation around each of the "I Am" declarations of Jesus in the Gospel of John. These honest and encouraging stories of brokenness, hope and new life bear witness to the power of the Gospel to change all kinds of people in significant ways. For the discerning pastor, there is a year's worth of great sermon illustrations to be found in these pages." - The Rev. Dr. Roberta Hestenes, pastor, educator and author of *Using the Bible in Groups*

"I thoroughly enjoyed reading *The Seven I AMs of Jesus*. It is extremely well done, inspirational, encouraging, and uplifting. I highly recommend this to anyone who wants to draw closer to Jesus." - Dave Wertheim, author of *Men U: Courses for a Transformed Life*

"I highly recommend this book. It provides a gentle roadmap to meeting one's needs by drawing near to Jesus. The power of this book lies in the stories of people who risked trusting God to meet their deepest needs. As you see yourself on these pages, you will find guidance, encouragement and hope to sustain and fill you." - Kim Fredrickson, MFT, author of *Building a Compassionate Relationship with Yourself*

"My time with *The Seven I AMs of Jesus* felt like a fifty day soak in the tenacious love of Jesus Christ and his astonishing power to change lives, even my own. Read this book and watch what happens!"   - Janet H.

*"The Seven I AMs of Jesus* will be revisited over and over again and eagerly given to others. The devotional/personal testimony/study format is an inviting & inspiring guide to personally knowing & connecting to The Great I Am."   - Cathy T.

"I just have to say thanks for *The Seven I AMs of Jesus* devotional book. It is so well written and makes the stories in the Bible come alive! My wife and I love reading it and the questions are helping us become more transparent and honest with God."   - Ken M.

"As small group leaders in search of studies that will draw, entice, inspire, stimulate, teach and grow our group, my wife and I have found all of that and more in *The Seven I AMs of Jesus*. We drew closer to Jesus every day as we related to the lessons & learned more fully who the Great I Am is and how He can meet our deepest needs."   - Scott T

# TABLE of CONTENTS

# Acknowledgements

A heart-felt thanks goes out to each of the amazing Jesus-followers who allowed us to interview them and share their stories in this book. Your journey with Jesus has inspired and humbled us. Thank you for your transparency and willingness to allow the rest of us to journey with you.

Thanks to Bayside West Community Church and Bayside Church of Plumas Lake, the two pilot churches who first took this series for a test drive. May God richly bless you as you have so richly blessed us.

Thanks to Teddi Deppner and Janet Hanson for coming to our rescue with some last-minute proofreading. Your time and attention have made this book better. We take full responsibility for any remaining errors.

Thanks to Linda's writer's group – Dee, Ginny, Barb, Vicki, Tammy, Rebecca, Lisa, Teddi, and Janet. Your feedback, insight and encouragement are a true gift from God.

Thanks to our sons, Nathan and Jeremy, for graciously allowing mom and dad to stay glued to our computer screens for days on end. Thank you for your support and patience, and for your willingness to fend for yourselves when we ran out of time to buy groceries. You boys are a delight to your parents!

Thanks to Linda's parents, Ralph and Virginia, who helped chauffer our boys, pick up pizzas and do a hundred other things to keep us going as we neared the finish line. We truly could not have done this without you.

Our biggest thanks goes to the Great I Am. We love you and are so grateful for the countless ways you have blessed our lives. We hope we made you proud.

# Where is God?  The Story of "I AM"

"Where did God go?" He had been the God of their ancestors Abraham, Isaac and Jacob. He had protected them from extinction during an extensive drought. He had given them most-favored status with the Egyptian rulers and free land in the fertile Nile River delta. God was good to them, with the emphasis being on the word *"was"*.

It had been generations since God revealed Himself to His people like He had revealed Himself to their ancestors. Sure, they had been protected. Certainly life had been good for them. They had prospered in the Nile Delta, and over the generations what originally had been a family of seventy had now become "exceedingly numerous." But times had changed.

A new dynasty had emerged in Egypt, a dynasty with no connection to Joseph, their ancestor who had brought them to Egypt and protected them. Under the new rulers, Hebrews were seen as a threat to national security. The new Pharaoh, eager to establish his dynasty and make a name for himself, recognized an opportunity and turned the Hebrews into a slave labor force.

Now the Hebrews were suffering under their forced labor. But that was the least of their woes. A great evil had been decreed against them. To keep them from growing even more numerous, Pharaoh had ordered the death of every newborn Hebrew male and made it the patriotic duty of every Egyptian to see to it that this edict was carried out. These were terrible times for the descendants of Abraham. Ages ago, God had been good to them, but where was God now?

Far out in the desert wandered a grizzled, solitary man. His skin was rough and leathery from decades of living in the desert. His face was wrinkled, at least what little you could see of it peeking out from his long, bushy and graying beard. He lived a difficult life, but that was okay. He was alive and he shouldn't have been.

He was a Hebrew, one of those children who should have been killed at birth. His mother, however, kept his birth secret. Then, when she could no longer keep his existence quiet, she placed him in a basket and set him afloat in the river, trusting him to the God who once was, but seemed to be no more. It was there in the river that the daughter of Pharaoh found him and adopted him as her own son, naming him Moses.

This grizzled man, who now wandered alone in the desert with only sheep to keep him company, had once lived a life of royal luxury. But that was decades ago, before he murdered an Egyptian and had to run for his life.

As Moses was growing up in Pharaoh's household, the tension between his Hebrew heritage and Egyptian upbringing grew stronger. It finally reached a breaking point when Moses witnessed an Egyptian brutally beating a Hebrew. In that moment, Moses snapped, and in anger he murdered the Egyptian. It's somewhat ironic that at the moment he fully embraced his Hebrew heritage, he had to run away from it.

Now Moses was leading his undernourished flock of sheep up a mountain in hopes of finding better pasture and an escape from the unrelenting desert heat. As he climbed, something caught his attention. He squinted as he looked in that direction. "That's odd," he thought. "That bush looks like it's on fire."

He looked to the right and left for signs of someone who would have started a fire, but saw no evidence of another living soul. He looked again. Now the bush was burning even brighter. "How could this be?' he wondered. "The bush should be burned up by now." Moses wanted to get a closer look. He didn't know it, but his next step was going to radically change his life.

That's the way it is in life – sometimes your next step will be a life-changer, but you don't know this until after you take it. Moses took a simple step, and suddenly a voice spoke.

"Moses!"

No one knows what Moses' response was to this sudden voice out of nowhere, but it's doubtful that "startled" would be an adequate description.

"Take off your shoes for the ground you are standing on is holy."

Moses didn't argue.

"I am the God of your father, the God of Abraham, the God of Isaac and the God of Jacob." In other words, "I am the God who *was*; the God of your ancestors."

God told Moses that He was aware of the suffering of His people and had heard their cry. Moses' eyes must have widened in shock when God said that He was sending Moses back to Egypt, back to the place of his failure, back to the person he feared the most – the Pharaoh – in order to secure the release of Pharaoh's slave force. Moses' head must have been spinning.

As the enormity of God's assignment for Moses began to sink in, one big question pounded in his mind. "What if I go to the Israelites and say, 'The God of your Fathers has sent me to you,' and they ask me, 'What is His name?' Then what shall I tell them?"

Modern English translations of scripture fail to capture the force and meaning of the question. Moses isn't asking simply for a name. God has already identified himself as the God of Abraham, Isaac and Jacob. Moses knows who is speaking to him. When Moses asks for a name, Moses is really asking God to identify His character and ability.

From the Hebrew's perspective, God had seemingly been missing for generations, possibly centuries. He is the God who *was*. Moses is concerned that the present day Hebrews would not be very confident in a God who had let them suffer. When Moses says, "What if they ask your name?" the meaning is, "What if they question your (and therefore *my*) authority?" The force of the question is a skeptical "What can God do?"

God seems to be sympathetic to the question. There were no peals of thunder or flashes of lightning, no "How dare you question God!" declarations. God's answer was simple and profound.

"God answered, 'I AM WHO I AM. This is what you are to say to the Israelites: 'I AM has sent me to you'" (Exodus 3:14). The meaning is simple. God is saying, "I am present!"

God went on, "Say to the Israelites, '*Yahweh*, the God of your fathers – the God of Abraham, the God of Isaac and the God of Jacob — has sent me to you.' This is my name forever, the name you shall call me from generation to generation" (Exodus 3:15).

Yahweh is a variant spelling of the Hebrew for "I am". However, in Hebrew the vowels were left out of the word Yahweh because it was believed that this name was too holy to pronounce. A rough English equivalent of the word would be YHWH. English Bibles simply translate the word as "LORD" using small capital letters. In Exodus 3:15, we see God adding this name to His title as the God of Abraham, Isaac and Jacob. In other words God is saying, "I am not just the God of the past. I am the God who is present. I have always been present. I AM!"

God is ALWAYS present! This is a profound statement.

Think about the implications. There is no place you can go where God is not present. There is no struggle you fight where God is not present. There is no temptation you face where God is not present. God is present in your marriage, in your home, and in your neighborhood. God is present in your schools. God is present in your work.

God is present in your failures and in your triumphs. God is present in your fears and your courage. God is present in your illnesses and your health. God is present when you are at your best and when you are at your worst. God is present in every step you take. Imagine how profoundly different your life can be if you are aware of and confident in God's presence? That is what this devotional book is about. It is about improving your awareness of, and confidence in, the I AM.

Now, fast forward to New Testament times. It had been 400 years since the last prophecies had been spoken in Israel – 400 difficult years. The glory and power of the nation was long gone. They had been conquered and ruled over by Babylonians, Persians, Greeks and now Romans. Once again, God was missing. The presence of I AM was no longer being experienced. God had become distant. Even His name was too holy and awesome to pronounce.

It was into this scene that a carpenter, somebody of no importance from the backwoods town of Nazareth, stepped forward and said "I AM." With these words, recorded in the Gospel of John, Jesus revealed himself as God, not a God who was distant and unapproachable, not a God who had nothing to offer, but the God who is present, a God who can meet our deepest needs, a God who can fill the empty places in our life, a God who can fill us with His presence.

Who is God to you? Is He a God who *was*? Is He a God who is missing? Is He a God who is distant or frightening? Is He a God who isn't big enough for the problems you face? Is He a mystery, a historical curiosity, a psychological crutch, a figment of imagination, a fairy tale?

Now consider this: Who are you? What is you greatest need? Do you feel a need to belong? Are you looking for a sense fulfillment? Are you spinning your wheels looking for some direction? Do you feel insecure? Are you bored? Do you feel like you haven't accomplished much? Are you looking for an opportunity to make a difference?

In this devotional, you will come to know the I AM, Jesus, as he reveals Himself to us in John's gospel. To those needing acceptance, Jesus says, "I am He." To those hungering for something more in life, Jesus says, "I am the Bread of Life." To those feeling lost, Jesus announces, "I am the Light of the World!" To those who feel insecure, Jesus tells us, "I am the Good Shepherd." To those who are hopeless, Jesus declares, "I am the resurrection and the life!" To those looking for a purpose, Jesus says "I am the Way, the Truth and the Life." And to those who are dried up and feeling insignificant, Jesus proclaims, "I am the vine."

We invite you to open this book each day to discover the presence of Jesus, the great I AM, and experience the profound difference He will make in your life.

# Let Jesus Fill Your Deepest Needs
# How to Use this Book

Over the next fifty days, we invite you to nourish your relationship with Jesus, to experience His presence and the difference His presence makes. When Jesus fills our lives, He fills our deepest needs. We are not talking about physical needs for food, water and shelter. We are talking about something much deeper, something that still aches inside of us and leaves us dissatisfied even when our physical needs are met. They are our needs for unconditional love and acceptance, a sense of fulfillment, direction in life, security, a second chance, purpose and significance.

Material items cannot fill these needs. Relationships cannot fill these needs. Thrills and adventure cannot fill these needs. People have tried from the beginning of time to use those ways to meet their needs without lasting success. These needs signal to us that there is something we hunger for beyond the physical, relational, and emotional. That something is God – a God who is present.

In his gospel, John presents Jesus as God, "who became flesh and made his dwelling among us" (John 1:14). Then, through a series of "I am" statements in John's Gospel, we discover the kind of God Jesus is. He is the God who is always in the present. He is the great I AM. Each of these statements reveals something different about the way we can experience His presence in our lives .

## WEEKLY THEMES
Each week you will dig into a new I AM declaration of Jesus, starting with a story that will provide some background to that week's I AM.

## DAILY DEVOTIONS
Each daily devotional will help you understand a little bit more about the

declaration and how it is relevant to your life. Each devotional includes a scripture passage for you to look up and read, some teaching and reflection on the passage, and a story from someone who has experienced the difference Jesus' presence makes in their life.

## TESTIMONIES

These testimonies are all true. They are from men and women from different walks of life and different parts of the country. They represent multiple ethnicities and range from teenagers to retirees. They are people like you. They are the people you work with, live next door to, and sit near at church – and Jesus is making a difference in their lives. Some of their stories will be about recent, dramatic changes Jesus has accomplished in their lives. Other stories are about the difference Jesus has made as a result of spending a lifetime walking with Him. Hopefully, these stories will inspire you and give you a window into some of the ways Jesus works in our lives. *(Note: If you are reading this book together with your family, you may want to read ahead to be sure the content is appropriate for your younger children.)*

## REFLECTION

To nurture and experience the presence of Jesus in your life, we recommend that you do the whole devotional for each day and not just read the stories. By reading scripture, you plant God's living and powerful word in your life. The reflection questions will help you engage with Jesus' presence and make the day's lesson real in your life. Be sure you take time to think about and act on these questions.

## THE SEVENTH DAY

A unique aspect of this devotional is the seventh day of each week. On that day you will find instructions for practicing a spiritual growth exercise. The exercises may take thirty minutes to an hour, possibly more if God is doing something special. The investment of time will be worth it. These exercises will help you experience Jesus as the I AM you have been studying about throughout the week. In most cases, these exercises are ancient. They have proven their value over centuries. You will be blessed if you do them and even more blessed if you continue to practice them after these fifty days are over.

## SMALL GROUP STUDIES

At the back of the book you will find small group Bible studies for each of the seven "I AM" declarations. As you study God's word together with others, you will go even deeper into God's word and experience even more of His presence, . It is through the community of believers that we all grow up into Jesus and become mature, being filled with the fullness of Christ (Ephesians 4:9-16).

## SHARE YOUR STORY

If Jesus is present in our lives, then we all have a story to share about the difference He makes. After reading all the stories in this book, we want to give you an opportunity to share your story. As you have been inspired by the stories of others, others can be inspired by your story. Please visit www.theSevenIAmsofJesus.com and share your story – and read the stories others have shared.

## THE SEVEN "I AMS" OF JESUS ALL-CHURCH SERIES

This book can also be used as a part of a series that ties this daily devotional and small group study book with seven weekly sermons, so the entire church can study together. Imagine the impact this can have on your church. To find out more about the campaign, visit our website at www.FaithAlive365.com.

# Week 1

# "I Am He"

She glanced out the door. The sun was already high in the sky, baking the dusty paths that wound through her village. While the rest of her village took a siesta, she wrapped a shawl around her head and prepared to go out.

The shawl covered her long brown hair so that all you could see was part of her face. In her youth, her face had been smooth and pretty. But now lines radiated out from the edges of her eyes, the result of hard labor and many years spent in the unrelenting sun. But there was something about her face that could not be explained by sun or labor. There was no sparkle in her eyes or hint of mirth around her lips. Her face betrayed a sadness born of rejection.

She grabbed her large clay water pot and headed through the deserted streets for the well outside the village. Day after day she made this trek, always during the afternoon heat, and always alone.

The other women in the village would go out in the early morning to get water before the midday heat. That was the sensible time to go, but she didn't want to be around the other women. She knew what they thought. She heard what they whispered a little too loudly when she came near.

"The woman's a tramp."

"Is it true? Five husbands? And none of them could stand her?"

"That man she's with now, she's not even married to him. She'll sleep with anyone."

The rejection and criticism had made her distrusting and cynical. In public, she was as tough as her sun-weathered skin. But in quiet moments away from watching eyes, she ached over the pain of her rejection and longed for someone who would value her.

But she couldn't show weakness. She was afraid that if she cracked even slightly, she would fall apart completely. And the sharp-tongued gossips...oh lord, what would they do if they saw her break down? Talk about fuel for the gossip fire.

So, she – a reject, a cast-off, a five-time loser – walked down the path alone, tough but weary. Then she hesitated. A man was sitting at the well. He looked Jewish. "That's just great," she thought, "there's nothing worse than a Jew to remind me of my rejection."

Jews considered Samaritans to be traitors to the faith (it's a long story). They had rejected the Samaritans in every possible way for so long that a simmering hatred existed between the two. It was astonishing that a Jew would even be found in Samaritan territory. Usually they would spend an extra day of travel just to go around Samaria rather than step one foot inside the country.

Fortunately, she didn't have to worry much about this man. He wouldn't bother to speak to her. Jewish rabbis made it a point of pride to never talk to any woman in public, and certainly not a Samaritan woman. It was yet another rejection to add to her pile.

Showing her tough exterior, she completely ignored the man as she walked up to the well and started to draw water. She assumed he was also ignoring her, as if it were some kind of contest to see who could do the best job of ignoring the other. But then..."Oh my God, did he just speak to me?"

Her life was never going to be the same.

# REJECTION

## In the Word

Read John 4:10-14 and Revelation 22:17

The woman at the well knew the pain of a lifetime of rejection. She was thirsty for acceptance and love but saw no hope of ever experiencing it. She was labeled. She couldn't escape who she was. Then one day she met Jesus. Their meeting wasn't by chance. Jesus had been waiting for her.

Jesus not only knew when this woman would be coming to the well, He knew everything about her. He knew every hurt, wound and rejection she had ever experienced. He knew she was thirsty and that He could offer living water – forgiveness from her past, a love that would heal her emotional scars, and a new life with new purpose that could start immediately. That's a drink that refreshes.

Jesus knows everything about you as well. On the cross He felt every wound, hurt, rejection and sin that's been done against you, and that you have done to others. And now He's waiting for you to come to the well of His life and drink His living water.

## Jenny Harmon's Story

Jenny is quick to share how unworthy she feels. "God has blessed me in so many ways – in fact, it's almost embarrassing to talk about all of the blessings. I feel so unworthy of them." Because of these deep feelings of unworthiness, learning to receive God's good gifts has been a journey for Jenny.

From the time she was a young girl, Jenny was told that she wasn't good enough. She was told to change and be more like someone else. "God wired me to be a feeler," she says, "and that didn't bode well in my family. I cried easily, and they would make fun of me for that." With emotion in her voice, Jenny admits that "I never felt loved for who I was. That planted seeds of rejection in my heart that I carried with me into relationships with friends and on into being a teenager trying to navigate the boy-girl thing."

But even though she struggled with feelings of rejection as a child, Jenny doesn't blame her parents. They were married very young – her mom was 16 and her dad was 17 when they got pregnant with Jenny's brother. "They were just kids raising kids, and they did the best they could with what they had to give," she shares. Jenny is amazed that they were able to keep their marriage together as long as they did, divorcing when she was nine. But although she's grateful for all they were able to give her, Jenny still sees the source of her self-esteem issues arising from the messages she received as she was growing up.

Deep inside, though, Jenny knew that what her parents were telling her was wrong. She attributes this awareness to her accepting Christ at a very young age. Her family didn't go to church, but they allowed Jenny to attend church with a neighbor family. They were "a vibrant, amazing, Jesus-loving, people-loving family," she says, "and they poured God's love into my life." They told Jenny about Jesus, and she immediately responded. "As soon as I found out about Jesus, I wanted him."

At the age of five, Jenny prayed to receive Jesus into her heart. She laughs now because she remembers thinking that Jesus was actually living physically in her heart. She pictured him on a tiny rocking chair, sitting in her heart and going everywhere with her. So, even though she had negative influences coming from her family, she carried with her the truth that God loved her.

Years went by and Jenny married Joel, a strong and loving Christian man, and together they started a family. As Jenny grew in her faith and healed from the wounds of the past, she was determined not to let her dad negatively effect her life any further, since he was always the one she struggled with the most. "I always loved my dad," she says, "but in his brokenness he was abusive in some ways." So Jenny would spend time with her dad, but she was careful to put boundaries on their relationship because he still had the ability to hurt her deeply.

At the age of fifty, her dad was diagnosed with the early onset of Alzheimer's. At the time, he was going through his fourth divorce, so he was all alone. Two years after the diagnosis, Jenny's brother died unexpectedly, leaving Jenny as her father's sole support. Jenny was willing to shoulder the responsibility of power of attorney, and she continued to visit him regularly, but she was unwilling to let him or his illness destroy the healthy place she was experiencing in her life and family.

His illness continued to progress over a number of years, and then one day as Jenny was driving in her car, she felt God speaking to her heart. "I knew it was totally out of His love for me," she recalls. "He told me that if I didn't do something quickly about my relationship with my dad, I would regret it for the rest of my life. After losing my brother, I knew that voice of truth was right. I regretted not spending more time with my brother and I knew I would regret it if I didn't do something with my dad."

So Jenny and Joel arranged for her dad to move in with them. Jenny felt confident that God was leading her to do this, but she had fear about telling her dad the plan. He had always resisted help in the past. She remembers being terrified the day she went to share the idea with him.

Normally, because of his illness, it would take her dad awhile to recognize people. But on this day he recognized Jenny the minute he saw her. "There you are," he said. "You're the one. You're the one I want. I love you. I love you more than anything else in the whole wide world." Jenny was floored. Not only was this type of sentiment uncharacteristic for her dad, but he had also been losing his ability to string together more than a couple of words at a time.

When Jenny told him that they would be selling his home and he would be coming to live with her family, he responded, "I'm so proud of you – that's a real good idea." Again, Jenny was blown away.

Most Alzheimer's patients tend to become angry and even hostile as their illness progresses. But Jenny's dad went the other direction, becoming kinder and gentler. From that day on, he never went back to being resistant or cranky. He continued to be loving.

Her dad only lived for another six months after he moved in with Jenny's family, but it was a sweet time for her – a true blessing from God. God gave Jenny a small window of time where her father was still able to verbalize his love and tell her the things she had always longed to hear him say. It brought deep healing. And in his final days she saw her dad reach out to God. Jenny is filled with hope that she will one day see him in heaven.

"I feel so unworthy," she says, "and that's the point. That's why I need Jesus as my Savior – because I *am* unworthy. I am God's child and He loves me and He's pouring out his blessings on me. And it blows my mind."

## Make it Personal

- Have you experienced a rejection in your life that still leaves a hole?

- How do you react when you are rejected? Have your reactions been healthy for you and those around you?

- How many different ways did Jesus show acceptance to the woman at the well? Do you feel accepted by Jesus? How does that influence the way you live?

- How do you view God? Do you live in fear of His rejection or in gratitude for His love? What difference does it make?

- How has Jesus spoken to you in this devotional time?

## Prayer

Dear Jesus, thank you for accepting me just as I am and offering your unconditional love, even though I don't deserve it. Please heal me from rejections of the past and help me to offer your acceptance and love to others today.

# COMING CLEAN

## In the Word

Read John 4:16-18, Proverbs 28:13 and James 5:15-16.

Technically, she told the truth – she had no husband. But she concealed the fact that she'd been married five times and now had a live-in boyfriend. Everybody in town knew. She probably single-handedly kept the gossips in business. But the stranger didn't need to know that truth. After all, he was treating her with respect, something she wasn't used to, so why ruin it?

But Jesus knew the truth. The woman listened in horror as He spelled it out for her. Then she waited for the punch line – the condemnation and rebuke that were certain to come.

There are few things more terrifying to us than transparency — taking off the mask and being seen for who we really are. Why are we so afraid? We know the answer. We're afraid that if people really knew us, they would dislike us. We might even dislike ourselves. So we put on our masks.

Yet as terrifying as transparency is, there is little that is more exhilarating than having someone know who you really are and still accept and love you. Suddenly you are free. The experience is life-changing.

Jesus had pulled the woman's mask away, yet there was no hint of rebuke, disapproval or judgment. What a different feeling it must have been for her to be known yet still accepted.

## Steve Padilla's Story

Early one morning, Steve opened up his garage and surveyed its contents. It was a disaster area, the result of years of accumulation without organization. As Steve looked around, he thought, "This is a picture of the condition of my soul." He decided that it was time to reclaim his life, and the place to start was in the garage.

Steve began pulling things out, organizing as he went, sorting out what needed to be kept and what needed to go. After hours of work, his garage was completely empty and swept clean. Everything was on the driveway, organized and ready to go neatly back into place. Steve felt good. He had just taken the first step to organizing his life…until he noticed the termites. He couldn't put anything back in the garage until the termites were dealt with. His organization project was stalled on the driveway.

That's when it hit him. Through his garage project, God was teaching him a lesson. Steve realized that his real problem wasn't a cluttered soul. His real problem was the termites in his soul – sin. But just like he had to get everything out of the garage to discover the termites, he was going to have to get his sins out into the open in order to get rid of them. With shattering clarity, he realized it was time for him to come clean.

From the time Steve first heard about Jesus as a young adult, he had fervently and passionately served Christ. But there was one part of his life that Steve had not yet allowed Jesus to transform. In fact, it never occurred to Steve that this was even an area of sin.

Steve was a people pleaser. He craved the acceptance and congratulations of others and made it his mission in life to make others happy. Steve found it virtually impossible to say no. His need to please became a burden in his life, but Steve didn't want to let this burden go. He craved hearing people say, "Good job."

As a musician, Steve loved using his talent to serve God and he experienced a lot of success. He toured the country with a Christian recording artist and loved it. "I felt like I was doing what God intended for me to do," Steve said. But there was a problem. He was working like crazy.

He was not only a member of the band, he was also its manager and promoter. In addition, he was a full-time church music director. People were telling him, "You're doing great. Keep it up," and would then ask him to do more. Steve was the "go to" guy who got things done.

Because he was serving God, Steve reasoned that "This must be what God wants. This is what I was made to do. I'm here to make others happy." In reality, he was burning out, but he kept pushing harder. He didn't want to let anyone down.

Steve discovered that drinking alcohol helped him pretend everything was okay, plus it gave him energy to push his limits. So, as people kept saying, "You're doing great...keep it up," Steve kept doing more. The harder he pushed, the more he would drink. But no one knew how much he was drinking because Steve had become adept at wearing a mask.

Eventually, Steve recognized he had a problem, but what could he do about it? He kept telling himself "I have to keep going, I can't let anyone down." The breaking point came when he got into an argument with a band mate, and no matter what Steve tried, he couldn't make that person happy.

Steve's whole identity was founded on making people happy. But on that day, for whatever reason, he was failing. That was the breaking point for Steve, and he went outside and sobbed. He finally realized that he couldn't keep going.

When he got home, he dumped out all of his liquor, joined Celebrate Recovery, and started taking the necessary steps to become sober. Then came the day he decided to clean out his garage and he realized he needed to come clean himself. The termite problem in the garage would have to wait until tomorrow. Steve had calls to make.

Steve had already confessed to his family, but now he started calling friends and coworkers. He told them about his problem with people pleasing, about his drinking and his deception. He asked for their forgiveness. "My friends and family responded with incredible graciousness," Steve says, "I felt like someone had just walked by and knocked an incredible burden off my back."

Later that evening, Steve returned home from meeting with some friends and saw that his son had cleared out an area of plants next to the garage and was pouring oil on it. His son, without being asked, had discovered where the termites were living and had worked all afternoon to pull out the plants so the termites could be destroyed.

Suddenly, Steve had another picture of what God was doing in his life.

Through his son's actions, God was saying, "Steve, as you admit your sin and get it out into the open, my Son will tear out the sin's bitter roots and destroy them." Steve got out of his car and gave his son a big hug and said, "Thank you. You've just given me the greatest gift of my life." Steve had just experienced God's grace in more ways than one.

Prior to that day, Steve thought he was working for God, but in reality, both his work and approval-seeking had become his gods. Ironically, while working for God, Steve had grown further away from God, until he opened up the garage door to his soul and came clean.

## Make it Personal

- Do you find it hard to confess your sins to another person or to admit that you did something wrong? Why?

- Is it possible that the masks we wear to keep other people from seeing the truth can also prevent God from transforming us? What mask might God be calling you to remove today?

- Why is church the place where we feel we have to pretend the most? Can the situation be changed?

- What has Jesus done that makes it easy to take off your mask with Him and come clean? What can you do to make it easier for others to do the same with you?

- Why is coming clean a relief? When is it not a relief? Do you need to come clean of something?

- How has Jesus spoken to you in this devotional time?

## Prayer

Dear Jesus, thank you for the forgiveness and freedom you offer. Please show me where I need to come clean today, and give me the strength to surrender my masks. Help me accept your forgiveness and live in the freedom of that forgiveness today. Amen.

# LOVER OF HER SOUL

## In the Word

Read John 4:1-42.

Unconditional love means we are loved with no strings attached. It means we will be treasured and cherished, protected and cared for, even when we fail. It means that there is someone we can always count on, who will believe in us even when we don't, who will listen to us even when we don't make sense. And when we succeed, they'll be cheering for us. Unconditional love is one of our greatest needs, and we all know it. We thrive when we experience it, and die a little each day when we don't.

When the woman at the well began to engage in conversation with Jesus, she experienced something that was foreign to her. This stranger noticed her, spoke to her, and treated her with respect. He didn't judge, sneer, curse, or ignore her. If she knew what unconditional love felt like, she would have realized it felt something like what she was experiencing.

Their conversation took many unexpected twists and turns, but the more they talked, the more she felt accepted. Did you notice the change in the woman? She left town a loner, but returned a leader. She had found the Messiah and the experience changed her.

## Jennifer Ferrell's Story

*NOTE: Some of the content in this story may not be suitable for young readers.*

"I'm done!" said Jen, "I want nothing more to do with Jesus." Jen was angry at God. And at the age of twenty, she took her anger out on Him by denying His existence. From that time forward, she turned her back on God, and if anyone asked whether she believed in Jesus, she would tell them she was a Buddhist just to end the discussion.

Jen's anger had been building for many years, fueled by the abuse she suffered at the hands of her father, who also happened to be a pastor. When she was only three years old, he began molesting her and using her to help him attract a series of girlfriends. But Jen was not the only one being tormented by her father's cruelty. Her mother was also a frequent target. Jen's father was angry all the time, often screaming at Jen's mother and severely beating her. Jen's only escape was to hide in the safety of her closet until the screaming stopped.

The abuse continued for several years until one day, when Jen was seven, her mother came home early from work and discovered her father in bed with Jen. That was the day she and her mother moved out of the house, but it wasn't the last time Jen suffered at the hands of her father.

At the age of twelve, Jen moved back in with her dad. It may seem strange that her mother would allow this, and that Jen would agree to it, but each of them had developed a powerful coping mechanism – complete denial. They never talked about the abuse, and each of them had actually blocked out or forgotten most of it (until many years later).

Now that Jen was back with her father, she was once again a target. If she did anything he didn't like – which was almost anything – he would use a leather strap to beat her until blood blisters formed. But he was calculating about the abuse. Because Jen was in cheerleading and wore short skirts, he was careful only to beat her on her torso so that the bruises wouldn't show.

One day, Jen had to come home from school because she was sick, which angered her father. So he began to deliver the lecture that always preceded a beating, saying, "This is going to hurt me more than it will hurt you." She interrupted by telling him she was about to throw up. He informed her that if she made any mess, she would be in so much trouble that she wouldn't see tomorrow. Jen was so afraid of her father that she threw up into her hands, trying to catch it all before it landed on the ground.

As horrible as her life was, things didn't come to a head until one night when Jen had a friend stay for a sleepover. During the night, Jen's father tried to molest her friend, and her friend didn't keep quiet about it. Soon the whole school knew. Jen was humiliated and traumatized. She begged her mother to let her come back to be with her.

For the next few years, life was relatively peaceful for Jen. Her mother had married a wonderful Christian man, and her new stepdad was a true father to her, showing Jen the kind of love she always longed for. During this time, Jen also began a relationship with Christ, going to church with her mom and stepdad. When Jen got married at the tender age of nineteen, her stepdad – or "real dad" as she calls him – walked her down the aisle.

A year later, when her first daughter was born, Jen decided to send a photo of her child to her biological father. He responded to the picture of his blond, blue-eyed granddaughter by sending Jen an angry letter. He said Jen's daughter was beautiful, but then called Jen a "half-breed" (since her mother is Japanese) and claimed that she had no business raising such a beautiful child. He told Jen she should give up her child before she ruined her. He then went on to make the outrageous claim that Jen needed to apologize to him for everything she had put him through, for tempting him and putting herself in front of him and making him do what he did. According to him, it was all her fault.

That was the day Jen walked away from God. She told God, "If that is who you have teaching your word, I want nothing more to do with you."

Even though Jen walked away from God, she can see now that He never walked away from her. For twenty years, God pursued Jen. Finally, after two divorces and an affair with a married man, Jen's life fell apart. Her anger and depression were consuming her. She felt empty, lost and lonely. In desperation over her brokenness, she realized that she needed to reach out for God.

So where did Jen go to begin the long journey back to God? The garage. She began searching through boxes in her garage for the Bible she once read as a young girl. After hours of searching, she found it – still covered with unicorn and rainbow stickers.

She plunged in and started reading straight through from the beginning.

And God began softening her heart. "When I reached Romans," she says, "I completely lost it. I cried through the entire book." At that moment, Jen's heart was cracked wide open to let Christ back in.

In the two years since that time, God has been doing an amazing work in Jen's life, bringing healing to the broken places and restoring hope for her future. Through a process of prayer, godly counsel, and writing a letter to her dad, she's been able to forgive her father for all the abuse and let go of the anger that had been holding her captive. She's also stepped out in faith and shared her testimony at Teen Challenge, encouraging others who have suffered abuse and showing them the path toward healing and hope.

Jen knows the journey is not over, but each day she is learning to embrace the forgiveness and love of Jesus – the true lover of her soul.

## Make it Personal

- When and where have you experienced unconditional love?

- How has the presence of unconditional love, or the lack of it, shaped you?

- Have you ever sought love and acceptance in unhealthy ways? Why are people an unreliable source for meeting our need for unconditional love?

- Do you believe it is possible to experience unconditional love from Jesus? Read these verses to learn about the love Jesus has for you: John 3:16, Luke 23:32-34, Romans 5:6-8, Isaiah 53:5, Ephesians 3:14-19.

- How has Jesus spoken to you in this devotional time?

## Prayer

Dear Jesus, thank you for your unconditional love for me. Help me to receive your love today and allow your love to heal and transform me into the person you created me to be. Amen.

# QUENCHING YOUR THIRST

## In the Word

Read John 4:7-29 again.

Jesus had the attention of the woman at the well. At first she tried to snub him. After all, Jews had snubbed her and her race for a long time. Then she got curious. Maybe Jesus knew of a spring that would be easier to use and have fresher water. But as the conversation progressed, she began to realize that she had a deeper thirst – a spiritual thirst – and that Jesus was offering spiritual drink that would quench her need forever. Could He really make good on His claim? He could, if he was the Messiah, the one they had been waiting for.

We know when we're thirsty. There's something deep down we desire. It might be a need for acceptance, a search for peace, or a desire for happiness. But no matter what we try, we just can't quite quench our thirst – until we realize that there's a spiritual cause for our thirst that requires a spiritual source to quench it.

## Julie Carson's Story

Lavinia had something that Julie wanted – peace. At work each day, Julie noticed that Lavinia seemed to handle the stress of life much more peacefully than other people. Julie was attracted to this, but didn't understand the spiritual source of that peace.

For quite some time, Julie had been on a spiritual quest. As a logical person, a thinker, things needed to make sense in order for her to believe.

To Julie, it made sense that someone must have created the world. It made sense that there must be some type of god out there.

For a long time, she identified with the idea of the "Great Spirit", from Native American religions. After going through treatment for a drug addiction, Julie began to use the language of Alcoholics Anonymous, calling on her "Higher Power." Her idea of God kept Him distant and somewhat impersonal. She wasn't ready to believe in the Jesus of the Bible – at least not what she knew of Him at the time.

But God kept planting seeds in Julie's life. First, He used Lavinia from work, and then He used a world religions course that Julie took as she pursued her bachelor's degree. In that class, Julie began to read up on all the major world religions. She wanted to figure out which religion was the right one. As she searched for truth, she came to the conclusion that the faith story that made the most sense was the story of Abram from the Jewish religion. "That's the story that went back the furthest," she says, "and made the most sense to me."

So one day at work, Julie told Lavinia, "I think I've figured it out – I think I'm going to be Jewish." Lavinia didn't judge her, but just listened. Occasionally, Lavinia would share about her own faith in Jesus, but Julie resisted, saying, "I don't like Him." It didn't matter to Julie that Abram was also part of the Christian faith story. She was okay with Abram and Judaism, but she wanted nothing to do with Jesus. After all, she reasoned, Jesus had let her down. He had let bad things happen to her including abuse as a child and a serious car accident as an adult.

Throughout this time, Julie continued to have spiritual conversations with Lavinia, telling her what she believed and what she wanted to believe, but just couldn't. Lavinia listened, and prayed.

Then God set Julie up for a divine appointment that would change her life. Julie was taking care of her grandsons one weekend and her daughter asked Julie to drop them off at Sunday school later that morning. When Julie took her grandsons to church, she decided that since she was already there she would stay for the service. Julie remembers what she did when she got home that day. "I called Lavinia up and told her I went to church. I think I heard the phone drop."

It just so happened that the church was in the middle of a series called "30 Days to Live." Julie was intrigued. The sermon caught her attention and made sense. So she came back the next Sunday and then the next Sunday. When that series was finished, they announced the next sermon series and that sounded intriguing as well. So, Julie kept coming. That was about a year ago, and she has continued to attend faithfully every week.

When Julie heard about a class being offered at the church about how science relates to the Christian faith, Julie decided she needed to attend. The class ended up being very helpful to Julie and her logical mind. It helped her make sense of the many questions she had about the interplay between science and faith.

After a few months of attending church, Julie reaffirmed her faith in Jesus – a faith she once had as a little girl. She's come to understand that the bad things that happened to her were not because God is not good. It is people who often are not good and they do bad things because God has given us the free will to make choices. Sadly, that freedom of choice can end up hurting others. But now Julie sees that through it all, God has been with her. His love has been constant.

Today, Julie is growing strong in her newfound faith. She and her friend Lavinia are doing a Bible study that was a part of the "30 Days to Live" series, working through the scriptures and questions together. Having a friend like Lavinia has made a huge difference for Julie in her journey with Jesus. It was also a joy to have Lavinia join her last summer at her baptism as she publically proclaimed that she is now a follower of Christ Jesus.

Julie is also growing by constantly asking her pastor theological questions. "I'm very picky about who I get my information from because I don't want to be led astray," she says. Julie's mind is constantly taking in information about God and the Bible, soaking it up like a sponge, and as a result her faith is getting stronger every day.

Now Julie is the one hearing other people comment on how peaceful she is. Just as she once noticed Lavinia's peace, Julie's friends now say they see a big change in her. She is handling stress much better, and she's no longer an angry person. She has become aware of Jesus' presence with her, helping her through tough times. "I've learned that God doesn't always change our circumstances," says Julie, "but He changes us." Her life is a testimony to that truth.

## Make it Personal

- Do you have a thirst you can't seem to quench? Might it have a spiritual root?

- Julie's journey towards a relationship with Jesus happened gradually. At first she just believed in a nebulous concept of a "higher power" and scoffed at the idea that Jesus was real. But slowly she became curious, then intrigued and finally committed. Where are you on your own journey? Where do you want to be?

- Read Psalm 42:1-2 and Psalm 63:1. What are David and the Sons of Korah describing? As you read, can you *feel* what they are describing? Have you ever felt that way about your relationship with God? Would you want to? Would there be a benefit to feeling that way?

- Read Proverbs 25:26. Are you missing out on Jesus' refreshment because you're "muddying" the waters? How are you doing it? When do you plan on doing something about it?

- How has Jesus spoken to you in this devotional time?

## Prayer

Dear Jesus, thank you for inviting me to quench my thirst in you. Help me to keep seeking you, learning more about you, and drawing close to you. Please reveal yourself more fully to me today. Amen.

# FINDING GOD

## In the Word

Read John 4:19-38 and Jeremiah 29:12-14.

As a result of being rejected by the Jews, the Samaritans created their own place of worship. It was yet another point of contention between Samaritans and Jews. By asking which location was the right one, the woman at the well was really asking, "Where can I go to find God?" It's an ancient question still being asked today. "Is there a God? Can I find God? How can I do this?" Where do we look for answers?

Jesus gave a two-part answer. First, Jesus said that finding God wasn't a matter of location but a matter of the heart. Then Jesus goes further, saying that to find God you don't go to a place, you go to a person – Him.

When Jesus says "I am He," He forces us to make a decision. Will we find God in Jesus?

## Bill Squire's Story

It was 1969, and the campus of UC Berkeley was the epicenter of the counter-culture. The college campus swarmed with anti-war protesters, hippies, Marxists, and just about every other cause, movement and cult in existence. Disenchanted with the status quo, youth were hungry for something different, something true, something that would counter the violence of a war far away and racism close at home.

Berkeley was the symbol of all things anti-Christian, or so many church going folk thought. But Bill and his friends saw an opportunity to share

Jesus with people looking for spiritual truth.

Bill and his friends didn't look like the typical church worker you would see in the 1960's. Instead of slacks, a buttoned-up shirt, polished shoes and short, cropped hair, they had long hair and beards, and they wore jeans, army boots, and army surplus fatigue jackets. In other words, they looked like hippies.

Bill spent his days walking around campus passing out pamphlets and talking to people about Jesus. He and his friends were trying to reach people who had dropped out of society and whose identity was wrapped up in proving they were different from the status quo. Since Christianity was considered part of the status quo, how effective could they actually be talking to disenfranchised college students about Jesus?

"It was phenomenal," Bill says. "Kids were hungry to find out about Jesus. Even hitchhikers were ready to talk about Jesus." Bill describes it as a time of revival where God's Spirit was moving strongly. "I was just lucky to be born at the right time so that I could be part of the movement."

There was no end to the creativity Bill and his friends used in introducing people to Jesus. For example, when Billy Graham came to Oakland for a Crusade, they started a group called "People's Committee to Investigate Billy Graham."

"We set up a table in Sproul Plaza, the main hub of campus where everyone hung out. We put a sign on it that said 'Investigate Billy Graham,' and we set out pamphlets both for and against Billy Graham. We did it to build up curiosity amongst a group that would otherwise completely ignore Billy Graham.

"When the Crusade started, we rented buses and put big banners on them that said 'Investigate Billy Graham.' We drove up and down the main campus street with bull horns saying, 'People of Berkeley, investigate Billy Graham!'"

By challenging them to *investigate*, Bill and his friends piqued the interest of people who prided themselves in being free-thinking. They ended up bringing packed buses to the Crusade and a number of those people walked forward and accepted Jesus.

As people started coming to Christ, Bill's group launched small group

Bible studies that met all over campus. They also bought homes where new Christians could live for a low cost and have fellowship. They even started Rising Son Ranch, a place where new believers who were leaving drugs, Transcendental Meditation, or other cults could go to get grounded in their new faith in Jesus.

Bill has plenty of stories to tell about young men and women whose lives were changed when they accepted Jesus as their Savior. For instance, there was Jeanie. "She was just a seventeen-year-old kid when we found her sitting in a gutter, lost and on drugs, and started talking to her." She accepted Christ and started to grow, Bill shares. "She eventually sang at our wedding and went on to become an attorney."

Another young woman, Laurel, had been part of a cult that had twisted a verse from the Bible about hating your mother and father. The cult leader had sent her home saying, "If you love Jesus you need to go home and prove your hate for your parents." Laurel destroyed her parent's home, ripping up furniture and breaking everything she could find in order to "show how much she loved Jesus."

Laurel showed up at a "Birthday Party for Jesus," hosted by Bill and his group at Christmas time. At the party, the staff heard Laurel's story and were able to show her the cult's errors and share with her the truth about Jesus. That night, she prayed to accept Jesus and quickly became a new person, and a new daughter, who was able to reconcile with her family.

Several years later, Bill heard about a need for furniture among many Mienh refugees living in East Oakland. So Bill got families from his church to donate used furniture. He would fill up his pick up truck and drive it to refugee neighborhoods in Oakland.

Bill didn't stop there. Next he brought his guitar and started singing simple camp songs to help the Mienh kids and adults learn English. The kids loved it. Inspired, Bill told his wife, "We need to do a Vacation Bible School." So they did a two-week VBS and 80 kids showed up.

At the end of the VBS, Bill asked, "Do you want to keep meeting?"

"Yes!" they all yelled enthusiastically.

So Bill started a weekly Good News club. Next Bill said, "These kids need a church." Soon Bill and his wife were moving out of Berkeley and into inner-city Oakland to help launch a new church.

Today, Bill is in his sixties, but he hasn't slowed down much. "If there's a lesson I've learned over the years of doing ministry, it's to think outside the box. Ministry doesn't just happen within the walls of a church. There are a lot of ways of reaching people with the good news." Bill is still thinking outside of the box, dreaming up ways he can share Jesus with those who are searching.

## Make it Personal

- What has your search for God been like?

- In the 1960's and 70's, some Christians dismissed the counter-culture as people who had rejected God and Christianity. But Bill saw a group hungry for spiritual truth and knew he had the answer. Are you confident that Jesus is the answer to our deep needs? Are you confident enough to tell others that Jesus is the answer they are searching for?

- What do you think it means to "worship in spirit and truth?" Does that relate in any way to seeking God with all your heart? How does God respond?

- Would you say you are seeking God whole-heartedly or half-heartedly? What's the difference?

- How has Jesus spoken to you in this devotional time?

## Prayer

Dear Jesus, please help me to keep seeking you and finding you. Break my heart for the things that break your heart, and help me to respond to others in love. Help me today to have eyes to see others who are searching for you, and help me share the truth about you with others. Amen.

# A NEW YOU

## In the Word

Read John 4:28-30, 39-42 and 2 Corinthians 5:17.

As you've read the story of the woman at the well this week, have you noticed the change in her? She was so excited about what she had discovered that she forgot she was a rejected loner. She went to the well in the heat of the day to avoid people from town, but after meeting Jesus she rushed off to talk to them.

The community changed as well. Thanks to the woman's testimony and enthusiasm, they came out to investigate, and believed for themselves that Jesus is the Messiah.

That's what happens when you believe in Jesus. His presence changes you and allows you to shed the baggage of the past so that you can become a new you.

## Deanna Dominguez's Story

Deanna's only religious experience came when she was eleven years old. Although her family wasn't religious, they would send her to the local Mormon church to "take care of the family's sins." While she spent three hours in church every Sunday confessing sins, the rest of her family would go to the lake. That lasted for a year. She figures that her parents must have decided she had confessed enough to take care of everything. So Deanna never went back to a church of any kind…until recently.

A year ago Deanna was going through a difficult divorce and custody battle. The pain of a failed marriage along with all of the lawyers, court dates, and worries about what was best for their two young daughters had spiked her stress level off the charts.

Something was missing in Deanna's life and she searched for answers everywhere. "I tried good ways and bad ways," she says, "but the bad ways were easier." To fill her ache for whatever was missing in her life, Deanna had turned to smoking. She also went bar hopping and had a string of sexual partners. But at best, these things only brought momentary relief. The ache, the longing, the searching were all still there. It depressed her that none of the things she tried were working, but like a broken record, she kept doing them over and over again because she didn't know a better way.

Then ten months ago, one of Deanna's girlfriends spent a Saturday night at her place. The next morning at breakfast Deanna's friend asked to be dropped off at church. For some reason Deanna said, "I can't just drop you off and leave you. I'll come to church with you."

Deanna hadn't been to church since she was eleven years old, but she didn't see any harm in going. She was actually a little curious about what goes on there. Little did she know that her decision was about to change her whole life.

Deanna still vividly remembers the message the pastor gave that morning. She remembers him talking about God's "agape" or unconditional love and how she needed to "let go and let God" deal with her struggles.

The pastor then took out a long rope and had people wrap it around the entire auditorium. He told people to imagine that the rope represented eternity. He then grabbed a section of the rope and wrapped a thin piece of tape around it, so thin Deanna couldn't see it from the back where she was seated. Pastor Chuck said, "This piece of tape represents your entire lifespan compared to eternity. So, why are you so stressed about what is happening now when you have all of eternity to look forward to?"

It suddenly all made sense. This was the answer she had been looking for her entire life, but had never found. When the pastor asked, "Why don't you let Jesus love you, forgive your sins, take charge of your life, and help carry your burdens?" she was ready to say yes.

Deanna experienced an instantaneous and eternal change the moment she said "yes" to Jesus. She suddenly felt clean and relieved of the burden of stress she had been carrying. Her ache, longing, and searching were gone. So were her coping mechanisms. She was able to immediately quit them all and she's never missed them. Jesus filled the void in her life and now she feels relieved to be free of the trap she was caught in.

Today her life is much more peaceful. She has learned to nourish her relationship with Jesus through prayer and Bible study. And when stress starts to build up in her life, she has learned to turn it over to Jesus in prayer and "let him worry about it."

Deanna has also noticed a difference in other areas of her life. "When I didn't get along with people, I used to react by gossiping and talking bad about them in order to make myself look good. That just made things worse. It led to tense work relationships which only added to the stress in my life." But that has changed since her life-changing Sunday morning.

Now, instead of gossiping and criticizing, Deanna prays about tense relationships and looks for ways to care and show love. In her words, "God listens" to her prayers and has helped her heal strained relationships. Her workplace no longer feels like a battleground, and she enjoys coworkers she used to dislike.

Deanna says that Jesus' presence feels "like a really BIG hug" that fills her with a feeling she finds hard to describe. The best description she can give is that it's a "warm and a calming presence."

Deanna hadn't been to church in years and then, on a whim, she walked into a church and one hour later came out a different woman. Does Jesus make a difference? Deanna will tell you that Jesus makes all the difference in the world.

## Make it Personal

- Is Jesus making a difference in your life? What kind of difference?

- The townspeople in John 4 said that they no longer believed because of what the woman had told them, but because they had seen and heard Jesus for themselves. Why is this distinction important?

- If you believe in Jesus, what are your reasons for believing?

- What happens when we commit our lives to Jesus? Do you believe that's true? Do you act like you believe that's true?

- How has Jesus spoken to you in this devotional time?

## Prayer

Dear Jesus, thank you for the new life you offer me. Help me today to allow you to keep changing me and making a difference in my life. Amen.

# ENTERING THE STORY WITH JESUS

## Preparation

Find a quiet, comfortable place to meet with God. Take a few moments to prepare yourself to hear from God. Shift your focus away from anyone who may be nearby. Relax your body and even close your eyes for a moment. Take a deep, slow breath and let go of the noise and busyness in your mind. Ask the Holy Spirit to teach you, protect you and guide your prayer. The Lord God delights in you, His precious child, and He has something special for you during this time.

## Entering the Story

Use "The woman at the well" story from John 4:4-42 for this exercise. *(Note: this is also a great exercise to use in the future with other stories about Jesus.)*

Read the story through SLOWLY AT LEAST TWICE. As you read, try to put yourself into the story. Picture the scene as if you were there. Don't try to analyze the passage. Rather, experience it. Allow yourself to become absorbed in what is taking place. How is each person feeling? What is each person doing? How are you feeling, and what are you doing?

You might identify with a character and "see" things through their eyes. You might find yourself assisting in some aspect of the story or you may simply find a vantage point from which to watch Jesus. Allow your imagination the freedom to "play out" the biblical story as you are led by the Spirit of God.

As you enter the story, try to focus on what you hear, see, smell and especially what you think and feel as you encounter Jesus. Pay attention to any internal resistance as you do this exercise. There are no "right" or "wrong" ways to encounter the text. Simply let yourself experience it.

## Reflection

Now that you have read and experienced the passage, take time to reflect on the following questions. You may want to write down your thoughts.

1. Take a moment and write down what you just experienced, felt, and thought as you entered the story with Jesus.

2. What do you sense Him saying to you?

3. What do you want to say to Him?

4. How might He be calling you to respond to Him today?

5. Finish with a time of resting in the arms of Jesus. Thank Him for His presence and listen for anything else you sense He might want to say. And even beyond words, simply rest in His presence and be aware of His powerful and unconditional love for you.

# Week 2

# "I Am the Bread of Life"

If someone had told him about it, he would have said they were lying. But he had been there and saw it for himself. With his own hands he helped deliver basket after basket of food to thousands of hungry people. Yet how could it be? There had only been a few loaves of bread and a couple of dried fish. But the pieces of fish and bread kept flying into the baskets from out of nowhere, and people kept eating until they were full. In fact, after everyone ate their fill, there was still food leftover. It was a miracle.

Twenty-four hours later he was still trying to digest (literally and figuratively) what he had experienced. He knew he shouldn't be so surprised. This wasn't the first miracle he had seen. But still, every time he thought he had seen it all, Jesus pulled off something even more impossible. What would come next? Healing a blind man? "Ha!" he thought, "that would be something to see." Then he laughed at his unintentional pun.

He looked over to where Jesus was standing. Once again, there was a large crowd surrounding him. What were they talking about? They seemed agitated and Jesus seemed to be unsuccessfully trying to make a point. His stomach growled. "Unbelievable," he thought, "I'm already hungry. I wonder if I can get Jesus to pull a sandwich out of thin air?" He smiled again and then stood up and moved closer to Jesus to find out what the commotion was about.

"What? Am I hearing that right? These people are asking for more bread?"

"Sure we saw the miracle and ate the bread yesterday," they were saying, "but we're hungry again. What else do you got? Really prove to us that you're the Messiah."

"Unbelievable," he thought as he shook his head, "What will it take to satisfy them?" His stomach growled again as he walked over to Peter. "Hey, all this talk about bread is making me hungry. When's Jesus going to take us to lunch?"

# Day 8

# FULFILLMENT

## In the Word

Read John 6:25-36.

The crowd had just experienced the feeding of the 5,000 the day before, and now they were hungry for more. The miracle was great, but that was yesterday. "Show us something else." "Wow us again." "Moses provided manna every day for forty years. Can you top that?"

In the same way, we always want just a little bit more. Just a little bit more and we will be satisfied. Just a little bit more and we will obtain that elusive thing called fulfillment. It all leads to a life of selfish, and often self-destructive, striving. At best, we end up filling our lives with stuff, yet we still never feel full-filled. Is it possible that we are looking to the wrong things for fulfillment? Is it possible that the fulfillment we hunger for comes from a different source?

The crowd wanted more bread. They had seen the physical miracle but missed the spiritual truth. When Jesus said, "I am the bread of life," He was saying that fulfillment has a spiritual, not a physical source. We are full-filled only when we are filled by the presence of Jesus.

## Steve Lindner's Story (Part 1)

When Steve got out of the car that morning his only expectation was to enjoy a round of golf. Instead, a journey was set in motion that radically changed his life.

Steve's friend had invited him to fill out a foursome. While on the first

47

tee, he heard his friend talking to the other guys about a group they were in together. Steve was curious. So as they golfed, Steve asked his friend about the group. "Oh, it's just a group of guys who get together to talk about their problems," his friend replied. "Why? Do you want to come?"

Steve was intrigued. Underneath his façade of confidence and success, he had too many problems to count. A group where he could talk about his problems with other guys might provide the help he needed. Should he risk trying it?

Up to that point in his life, Steve had been living a selfish, prideful life. He would use anyone and do almost anything to get ahead. It didn't matter if he lied, did something unethical, or even hurt people – so long as it got him what he wanted. He thought that a "me first" attitude was the only way to get ahead in life, but instead, it was destroying his life.

Steve brought his "me first" attitude into his marriage. His wife and kids weren't a priority. The success he was experiencing at work fed his ego more than his family did, so work became his priority. His family was not as important as his pursuit of success and the happiness he thought success would provide.

"Thanks to me, my family was dysfunctional," Steve shares. "But since life was all about me, I no longer wanted to be part of the dysfunction I created. So, I left my family behind."

After awhile, Steve remarried. Before the marriage, he said to his fiancée, "You know how I am. So, by marrying me you're accepting who I am without expecting me to change, right?" She said, "Yes." But since life was still all about Steve, his new marriage was destined for the same outcome as his first marriage. Within six months of the wedding, they were in counseling.

The dysfunctional family Steve had left in his wake, and the struggles of his current marriage, were only the beginning of his problems. Added to that were all the lies he had told along the way to get ahead. All that deceit had now become a giant boulder teetering precariously over his head. One slip, one lie exposed, and his whole life could come crashing down. It had become exhausting to maintain all those lies. So, Steve came up with a plan.

Steve decided that the best way to deal with all his problems was to run away from them — literally. He bought property far from his home where no one knew him. By moving there, he reasoned, he could distance himself from all his lies and start fresh. But a question kept nagging at him. "Once you get there Steve, what then?" His subconscious was trying to tell him what should have been obvious. His real problems were internal and they would follow him wherever he went.

So, when Steve heard about a group of guys who met to talk about their problems and was asked if he wanted to come, his first thought was, "yes!" But what he said out loud was a more subdued, "I might give it a try."

The next morning, his friend picked him up and took him to an office complex where twelve guys were gathered. They opened in prayer and then started talking about what God was doing in their lives. Steve wasn't prepared for that. "They've sprung Amway on me," he thought in shock. "My friend has pulled a bait and switch." Steve would have never agreed to come if he knew that this was a faith-based group.

However, he was stuck there because his friend had given him a ride. So he listened, and once he realized they weren't trying to sell him anything, he became captivated by the sharing.

He started attending the group every week, and when his friend asked if he wanted to go to church with him he said "yes" to that as well. As Steve describes it, it wasn't long before "God started turning me inside out."

Four months went by, and one day Steve found himself on an elliptical trainer at the gym, reading the book *Man in the Mirror*. He was reading a chapter about having a personal relationship with Jesus, and it struck him, "I don't think I've ever had that kind of relationship." He reflected on that for the rest of the day, and then the next morning, while he was in the shower of all places, Steve prayed and committed his life to Jesus.

Steve has become a completely different man since then. His selfish, prideful, "me first" ways were thrown out as he started to follow Jesus. "Now I'm a better husband, a better father, and a better businessman," says Steve. "I can't imagine having a better marriage or better friends."

Prior to following Christ, Steve used people to help himself get ahead. Now, he serves people to help them get ahead. "I never gave even a dime to help out anyone," he shares. But now Steve leads the way in helping his church serve the community, from feeding the homeless to serving local schools. Serving has given Steve a joy and peace he tried to find with his "me first" approach to life but could never obtain.

The ripple effects of Steve's transformation have also transformed his family. Steve was sad about the fact that he had long ago burned the bridges between him and his children. He had little hope of helping them past the dysfunction he had created in their lives. But the change in Steve's life created a change in his relationship with his children, and now Jesus is making a difference in their lives as well.

Steve wants people to know that, "No matter what you've done, it's never too late. If God can wait patiently until I was fifty years old and then take someone as evil as I was and radically transform me, then I'm here to tell you it's not too late for you. God can also transform your life and use you to help transform the lives of others."

## Make it Personal

- How have you tried to obtain fulfillment? Or maybe another way to ask the question is: what are you trying to fill your life with?

- Do you have your own version of a "me first" attitude? In what areas? What damage has it caused?

- Bread is a basic staple of life. It is called a "filler". What can Jesus, the Bread of Life, fill your life with?

- Do you need to make a change in your approach to being fulfilled? Why? How will you do it?

- Do you have a personal relationship with Jesus? If not, turn to page 219 to find out how you can have this kind of relationship.

- How has Jesus spoken to you in this devotional time?

## Prayer

Dear Jesus, I know that fulfillment can only be found in you. Please help me live out the truth of that today, and seek you first in everything. Amen.

# FILLING THE VOID

## In the Word

Read Ecclesiastes 2:10-11, Ephesians 4:17-19 and John 6:35.

The Jews surrounding Jesus had just seen a miracle, and it was great – but the thrill didn't last. Now they wanted more. "Give us another thrill," they seem to be asking. Their attitude reflects this truth: experiences, however thrilling, die out in time. So do material objects, and even life itself. And as the experience fades, we are left feeling empty again, so we chase after more things and more thrills. After all, what choice do we have? If we are unaware of the presence of God, material things and emotional surges are all we're left with.

## Brien Whitlock's Story

Brien spent his life looking to fill a void he felt inside – and in the process, he messed up in just about every way possible.

As a rebellious teen, he tried to find friends and identity in all the wrong places. He dabbled in drugs, tried drinking, then graduated to stealing cars. He was constantly in and out of youth detention. When finally faced with the prospect of doing hard time in prison, Brien straightened up, broke with his friends, and landed a full-time job, but the void was still there.

Brien turned to making money and buying "goodies" in his continued effort to fill the void. He filled his life with stuff, yet the void still remained. In time, Brien fell in love and married. Surely a wife would fulfill his needs, but as great as his wife was, marriage still wasn't enough.

Brien then tried danger and thrills. He started motorcycle racing, zipping around race tracks at speeds exceeding 120 mph. At first, the danger gave him a buzz and seemed to fill his need. But as he advanced through the professional ranks, what had been a fun weekend hobby turned into work.

While racing one weekend, he went for a pass to take the lead. At 100 mph Brien lost control of his bike and slid 50 feet before crashing into a wall. He was able to walk away, but suffered a massive concussion. He was lucky—just the day before another racer had been killed in a similar crash.

That was the end of Brien's racing, but his search for fulfillment continued. He had an affair, divorced, married again, and then his second wife left him. He was making a mess of his life, but no matter what he tried, nothing filled the emptiness inside. To handle his stress and depression, Brien started drinking heavily.

It was during the turbulence of his second marriage that Brien started attending church. Some friends told him that it had helped them, so Brien figured it couldn't hurt. While he was in church, Brien says, "I could sense the presence of God." But when he left church he was still the same guy with the messed up marriage and a big drinking problem. Brien may have been committed to going to church, but he had yet to make a commitment to following Jesus.

Things continued to get worse. After his wife left, Brien's drinking hit an all-time high, and he started thinking it might be easier to end it all. He had a handgun in a safe at home and he would stare at that safe and wonder, "What if...?"

Scared by his thoughts, Brien started praying to a God he barely understood. "God, I know you have a plan for my life, but I don't understand what's going on. I'm in pain. I feel alone and alienated. I can't continue like this."

For days Brien wavered back and forth between thoughts of suicide and thoughts of God. Then one day while he was praying, he sensed God speaking to him. It was not a voice. It was more like an impression or a thought in his mind that said, "I'll give you strength if you give me commitment."

Brien realized that commitment was the step he had yet to take. Although he had gone to church, that was not the same thing as being committed to following Jesus. In fact, at this point he had even stopped going to church. That day Brien said, "Yes Lord, I will give you my commitment."

Brien kept his word. He quit drinking and started attending church again. He asked a strong Christian friend at work to mentor him. And during his long commutes, he listened to Christian teachers on the radio. Brien was filling his life with godly things, and inside Jesus was transforming him.

Brien started to let go of long held resentments. He became less demanding and more understanding. He started to become forgiving. As Brien describes it, his whole outlook changed. He noticed that things that had once made him angry no longer bothered him. Best of all, Brien says, "I no longer have that feeling of hopelessness."

Life didn't suddenly become a walk in the park for Brien. He is still cleaning up the messes he made, but now he has a new outlook and a new strength for dealing with his problems. And because he is trying to faithfully honor Jesus, Brien is not making new messes (or at least not as many).

Jesus is making a real difference in Brien's life, a difference that is obvious to him. He can't believe the changes. "The void is being filled up!" he shares excitedly. "I just wish I hadn't waited so long."

## Make it Personal

- Brien was driven by a desire to fill a void in his life. In what ways are you driven?

- What kind of messes have you made in your effort to fill a void in your life?

- In Ephesians 4:19 Paul talks about the difference between sensitivity and sensuality. What is the difference between them? Why does a lack of sensitivity only leave us with sensuality, and why does Paul say this leads to bad things?

- In today's passage from John, when Jesus says that you will never go hungry or thirst again, what is He referring to?

- What do you want to stop hungering and thirsting for? Do you think that the hunger will subside as you become more aware of Jesus' presence?

- How has Jesus spoken to you in this devotional time?

## Prayer

Dear Jesus, thank you for being the one who can fill the void in my life. Help me to recognize that only in you will my hunger and thirst be satisfied. Amen.

# NO EARNING REQUIRED

## In the Word

Read John 6:27-29 and Ephesians 2:1-10.

The crowd wanted to know what they needed to *do* to earn God's favor. That same question continues to persist today, subtly poisoning our relationship with Jesus. "What are God's requirements?" we want to know. "What do I need to do to please Him – or appease Him?" We can hardly be blamed for thinking this way. That's the way the world works. We get what we want when we do things others approve of. But that's not the way God works.

Jesus' answer was almost incomprehensible to the requirement-minded crowd. "You need to do nothing. The only 'work' required is to believe in me."

God's love, forgiveness and salvation cannot be earned. If we could earn it by our own effort, there would be no need for Jesus to come, no need for a crucifixion and no need for a resurrection. But there is no earning with God, only loving. When we are swept away by God's love, and moved to love Him in return, everything else will take care of itself. Instead of living in fear of God as we strive to measure up, we will experience freedom through God's love.

## Linda Sommerville's Story

Growing up as a tender-hearted people pleaser, I was always seeking approval from the important people in my life – mom, dad, teachers, coaches, youth leaders. But the one person I worked hardest to please was God.

Somehow, I developed the notion that God was like a parent I could never please. So I kept trying harder and harder to make Him happy. If there was a service project to participate in, I jumped in and worked harder than anyone. If there was a church event to attend, I made sure to come – and bring friends along, too. If there was a spiritual discipline to practice, I worked hard to "do it right."

In my early 20's, God began to break my heart for the many people in the world who need to know Jesus – especially those in other countries who don't have as much access to hearing the Gospel as we do in the United States. So I went on a short-term mission to the Philippines.

It was a challenging summer, including continuous tropical heat rash, a cockroach infestation in my room, language barrier issues with my Filipino host family, and times of intense loneliness. But it was also a summer of great fruit in ministry, with many people responding to the message we were sharing – and I felt sure God must be pleased with the hard work I was doing for Him.

When I returned, I began to think God might be calling me to a life of service as a missionary in a third world country. That seemed like the hardest thing I could do for God, and it made sense that this would be exactly what God would want from me. After all, my deepest desire was to please God.

Before heading back overseas, I knew I needed more training, so I enrolled at Fuller Seminary. While I was there, I met my incredible husband, Phil. But something else happened as well – God rocked my world.

I'll never forget the two-week intensive class I took on Church Renewal and Worship. Through hours of worship and teaching, I began to hear from God in new ways. And the message I was hearing was radical.

I sensed God telling me that He loves me. That by itself wasn't a new message, but God had more for me. Night after night, God increasingly impressed upon me that there wasn't a single thing I could do to make Him love me any more than He already did. No matter how many hard things I did for God, it couldn't possibly make Him love me more. And even if I never did another single thing for God for the rest of my life, it wouldn't make Him love me any less.

That blew my mind! Or more accurately, it cracked open my heart. That's because I had known these things for years. But somehow, I wasn't experiencing in my heart what I knew in my head, until I took that class.

I began to see that God didn't need me on the mission field. God didn't need me to reach the world for Christ. In fact, God didn't need me to do anything. But He wanted me. All of me. God began to woo me and allow me to feel how much He loves me. That love changed me – it changed how I saw God and how I saw myself.

I won't say that I was instantaneously cured of my intense need to earn God's approval, but I began to be a different person. And I began to learn how to simply receive God's love, whether I felt worthy of it or not.

For a number of months after that class, I wrestled with my sense of calling to ministry. Was that calling simply my own need to please God? Or was it truly God's purpose for my life to be in full-time ministry? I continued to take classes and grow in my awareness of God's love for me, and gradually I began to notice my motivations for ministry were changing. Instead of trying to earn God's approval, I found myself responding out of love for Him.

This was new. It felt completely different. Instead of being a driven, workaholic for Jesus, I found my heart being drawn to Him and His people. And in the process, I began to discover that God has indeed called and wired me for ministry. He just wants me to live out that calling from a place of love, not striving.

In the years that followed, I continued to do what some people might consider "hard things" for God, including working with inner-city kids for a summer in Philadelphia and planting a new church in Wichita, Kansas with my husband. I won't say I never struggled again with a need to earn God's approval, but my motivations for serving continued to change. Instead of trying to find the hardest thing I could do for God, I began to listen for His stirrings in my heart, paying more attention to what kinds of activities and ministries brought me life, and which were more draining.

Now, I meet one-on-one with people in a ministry called "spiritual direction." As a spiritual director, I help others listen deeply to what God is saying and doing in their lives. Often, I am able to pass on the message that God loves them. Period. No earning is required.

This ministry has been an unexpected gift from God. It's been a life-giving ministry that has given me a front row seat to watch how God's love changes hearts and lives. And as I help others, I experience something better than God's approval. I experience Him filling me with his love – a love that continues to change me.

## Make it Personal

- In what ways have you tried to earn God's favor? What feelings did this experience raise in you?

- What would it be like to have Jesus look you in the eye and tell you that the only thing He wants from you is to believe in Him and love Him? What kinds of striving behaviors might this free you from?

- In what way is the "work" Jesus calls us to (see John 6:29) different from the kind of work the world generally asks from us?

- Consider memorizing Ephesians 2:8-9. What is the difference between doing good works from a place of love and grace, and doing good works from a place of trying to earn approval?

- In what ways have you experienced the love of God? How might you rest in that love today and allow God to free you from the burden of trying to be "good enough?"

- How has Jesus spoken to you in this devotional time?

## Prayer

Dear Jesus, thank you for your unconditional love for me. I know I can never be good enough to deserve or earn that love. But I receive your love today and ask that you help me to respond to you by believing in you and following you with all my heart, mind, soul, and strength. Amen.

# PROOF

## In the Word

Read John 6:1-15, 28-38.

The crowd wanted more proof before they believed in Jesus. They had a "We-won't-believe-until-you-show-us-more" attitude. But Jesus had already shown them a sign when He fed the 5,000 with only a few loaves and fish. The miracle was proof that Jesus is the Bread of Life. Their problem wasn't with seeing – it was with believing.

Some of us have a hard time believing as well. We come to God kicking and screaming before we believe. Even as followers of Jesus we kick and scream when God says to forgive, or turn the other cheek, or treat others better than yourself, or give a "tithe" of 10% of your income.

How many "signs" do you need to see before you will trust Jesus? Maybe our problem isn't with seeing – it's with believing.

## Roger Baker's Story

In Roger's family, every weekend was like "Saturday Night at the Fights." His mom and dad would scream and throw things at each other until the floor was littered with shards of broken glass. "There were three doors in the house," Roger says, "and when the yelling started, me and my two brothers would run to get behind one."

"My family life was horrific. Our home was a disaster," Roger remembers. "We had to sleep with one eye open all of the time, and we always had to watch our backs because we never knew what was going to happen." As a result of such a chaotic and violent home life, Roger never had any peace of mind. He was always on edge, always angry, and always ready to blow up at people for little reason.

"Then, my mom became a Christian," Roger remembers. "Lord knows how she found Jesus. I never knew, but she found Him, and it was real." Roger's mom had been battling cancer, so he suspects that during that ordeal, someone told her about Jesus and she was ready to believe.

"I remember that after she found Jesus, she wanted to tell everyone she could about the joy and peace of mind she had discovered," Roger says. "Naturally, she wanted to save us, her children." But Roger didn't want to have anything to do with Jesus. So he and his mom start arguing (it was, unfortunately, the family's most familiar form of communicating).

"But Roger, I want you to go to heaven," his mom would say.

In his response, Roger was both rude and mean. "I don't want to have anything to do with God. I don't believe in God. Just stay away from me with all of your Jesus garbage!"

In the heat of the argument his mom quoted the scripture that said "Every knee will bow, and every tongue confess that Jesus is Lord" (Philippians 2:10-11).

Roger then shot back, "Listen woman, I am not bowing to anyone, especially not to some invisible God! If you want to be a Jesus freak, that's your choice!'"

"I was a terrible son," Roger admits. "I didn't even have enough respect to call my mom 'mom'. I remember her saying that she was going to pray for me until God revealed himself. 'Don't bother,' I replied and then left in a heated rush, slamming the door behind me."

However, Roger couldn't get the words "every knee will bow" out of his head. He was determined to make sure that he never gave his mom the satisfaction of seeing him on his knees. It sounds crazy, but Roger remembers paying very close attention to making sure that his knees never touched the ground for any reason. For the next several months, as Roger tried not to get on his knees, his anger towards God grew stronger. "I didn't believe in Him, nor did I ever want to," he says.

When Roger was eighteen, there came a day when the fighting between his parents became especially violent. His dad had thrown his mother to the ground and had a death grip around her throat until she started turning blue. Roger and his brothers reacted by doing what they always did, they ran for the doors. Roger ended up in the backyard.

"I couldn't take it any longer. Even though I treated my mother horribly, I loved her dearly and I was scared for her life," he shares. "I raised my fist towards heaven and screamed as loud as I could, 'IF YOU'RE SO REAL, PROVE IT!'"

"Then I heard a small voice inside my head say, 'Look down.' 'WHAT!?!' I literally screamed back towards heaven. "Again I heard a small gentle voice telling me to look down. When I did, I gasped in shock. I was on my knees.

"I immediately tried to get up, but no matter how hard I tried I couldn't get off of my knees. Right then I realized that my mother was right. There was a God, and He is sovereign. So there on my knees, I gave my life to Jesus and never looked back."

In that moment, Roger says he felt an enormous release. "Like someone had come by and knocked an enormous weight off of my back. Living in that home environment, I never knew peace of mind, until then. I sensed Jesus telling me, 'Everything is going to be okay.'"

Roger's new life with Jesus was a struggle at first. He started reading the Bible, figuring that if it was God's instructions he ought to read it. Then he thought, "I've got your book, God, now I want to find out about your people." He remembers going to church with his mom, but he didn't like it and sat in the corner scowling.

Then one Sunday, a woman just a couple of years older than him saw him sulking in the corner and introduced herself, asking how he was doing. Not wanting to talk to or even meet anyone, Roger snapped back, "Why don't you get the hell out of here!" He thought that would get rid of her. It didn't.

She stood her ground and they started arguing (again, the only real way Roger knew how to communicate). She ended up inviting him over to her house for dinner. "Get lost, there's no way I want to come to your house for dinner and hear you talk about Jesus." Again, she stood her ground.

"What?" she asked, "You mean you're afraid to talk to a little woman like me?" He couldn't turn down that challenge, so he showed up a few days later, ready to get into a full-blown argument. When he rang the doorbell, a sweet nine year old girl, a sister, answered. Roger melted. There would be no argument.

The woman became a good friend and mentor to Roger. She and others began to retrain Roger on how to live. They showed how different the life Jesus offered was from the life he had always known. And slowly but steadily, Roger grew out of the painful life he had experienced and into the loving life of Jesus

Today Roger has a heart for helping other new believers. "I remember how hard it was for me to begin this new way of living for Jesus," he remarks, "so I want to help others get off to a good start."

You may wonder what happened to Roger's family. His mom passed away and is waiting for him in heaven, and his dad and brothers have all put their faith in Jesus. Today, Roger and his dad are best friends. The verse Roger's mom quoted and trusted from Philippians that "every knee will bow" has come true in the Baker family.

## Make it Personal

- What "signs" has Jesus shown you of His presence?

- In what ways, or areas of your life do you sometimes resist believing Jesus? Why?

- Read Philippians 2:5-11. What is the significance of bowing your knee to Jesus? What does it mean? How much trust would you need to have to take this action? How did Jesus set the example? Does that help you trust Him?

- How has Jesus spoken to you in this devotional time?

## Prayer

Dear Jesus, thank you for the many ways you reveal yourself. Please give me eyes to recognize you today in the big and small miracles you send my way. Give me faith to believe you are truly God. Amen.

# BETTER THAN BREAD

## In the Word

Read John 6:47-51 and Romans 6:1-14.

The crowd wanted bread. But Jesus was offering something far better – eternal life. That is a "bread" that fills our greatest need. But something gets in the way of our receiving eternal life – sin. As long as our life is filled with sin, it can't be filled with God's gift of life. But there is a solution. Jesus died to pay the penalty for sin so that we can be forgiven.

When we believe in Jesus, He will remove the sin that clings to us and clogs our soul. Our sinful life is crucified with Jesus and the sin is removed. Because the sin is removed, we can begin to live a new life powered by God. You can think of this new life as your first taste of eternal life.

## Tye Sullivan's Story

He was picking his way along the factories and warehouses, sticking to the shadows. It was night time. In the distance he could hear sounds of fighting. Explosions rocked the city. As he passed a storefront, he looked into the large plate glass window and saw his reflection. It was shocking. He was completely covered in a gritty, black sand, dark as tar and just as sticky.

Up ahead was his target; it was a hilltop, and somehow he knew he needed to get there, but he didn't exactly know why. He just sensed that his life depended on it. Throwing caution to the wind, he began running towards the hill and then up it. As he looked up, he could see, standing on the hilltop, the figure of a man. It looked like...Jesus. If he thought about it, he would have realized that was weird, but in the dream it seemed normal.

He continued struggling up the hill. It was difficult climbing, but for some reason he knew that he needed to get to that man. It was a matter of life and death. When he reached the top of the hill, he noticed that the man was standing in a pool of water. As Tye stepped towards the man, he tripped and tumbled into the water.

The pool wasn't deep, and he quickly jumped back up to his feet, sputtering. But as he began to sweep back his wet hair, he froze. His eyes stared at the backs of his hands, then slowly looked down his arms, and then down the rest of his body. The black grit was completely washed away!

Tye woke up with a sudden start. He had been dreaming. But he had never had a dream like this one. Even now that he was awake, he could remember every vivid detail. Tye knew with certainty that the man he saw in his dream was Jesus, and that the tar black sand was his sin clinging to him. What was Tye supposed to do with a dream like that?

Tye hadn't been to church in forty years. He only had vague childhood recollections of the church his family attended. Like Tye, his wife Lori had grown up in church, but had also stopped attending decades ago. Although they both identified themselves as Christians, they never felt the need or desire to participate in a church or even explore what being a Christian meant. It seemed irrelevant to them.

Then Tye had this very real dream about his sin and Jesus. The message seemed clear – Jesus wanted Tye to come to Him and have his sins washed away. Why else would he have a dream like that? But still, what was he supposed to do about it?

Tye did what many of us would do when we are uncertain. He did nothing. He sat on it. But he didn't forget. In the background of his mind, Jesus was calling.

Tye had other things to worry about. He was unemployed, one of the countless victims of the recession. His wife had a job, but money was still tight. Their financial woes were a constant source of worry, and it was causing stress in their lives and tension in their marriage.

Tye and Lori were living in a brand new town. If you can picture someone taking an entire town and plopping it down in the middle of an empty field, you'll get an idea of where they live. It's a town of 7,000 people, but is so new that it only has one store, a Walgreens, and it only has one church that meets at the school.

At the edge of town, near the entrance to the freeway, you can find a small yard sign that advertises the church. Several times a week, Tye would drive by that sign on the way in and out of town. Finally, six months after his dream, Tye and Lori decided to check out the church. It was Easter Sunday.

It had been decades since Tye and Lori had been in a church, so they didn't know what to expect. They entered cautiously, but quickly decided they liked it. But they were wary of getting sucked into some kind of loony cult. So before leaving that Sunday, Tye wrote on a visitor's card, "I'd like to meet with a pastor." Tye wanted to find out what this church believed.

Before the week was over, Tye found himself having coffee with John, the church's Executive Pastor. Tye shared a little of his story and then waited to see how John would react. John was understanding; he showed no hint of condemnation, but he shot straight.

He told Tye, "Jesus wants to have a relationship with you, but you have put Him on the shelf for the past forty years. You shouldn't be surprised that you're not handling the stress well. You've said that Jesus is the Savior of your life. Well then, it's time you make him the anchor of your life as well."

That was the challenge Tye needed to hear. He suddenly realized that there was more to believing in Jesus than being saved from hell. Jesus could be present and making a difference in his life now. So after skipping church for forty years, he and his wife haven't missed a Sunday in the last four months. Everything is still new to them, but they are learning how to make Jesus their anchor.

Although little has changed in Tye and Lori's financial struggles, they've noticed that they are less stressed. Tye says, "Life's troubles are not as consuming as they used to be."

A few weeks ago, Tye was baptized. It was a concrete action that reminded him that when he put his faith in Jesus, the black tar of sin clinging to his life was washed away. Now as he looks back at the forty years he spent away from God, Tye remarks, "What was I thinking? I could have been enjoying this kind of life years ago."

He is so excited by his new life in Christ that he says, "I'd like everyone to know that there's no time like the present to begin your relationship with Jesus."

## Make it Personal

- Tye's dream pictured the sin as a tar-like sand that clung to him. How do you picture sin in your life?

- In today's passages, when Jesus says "this bread is my flesh," what do you think He is alluding to? In what way is His flesh bread?

- Romans 6 offers a great picture of what happens at the moment we commit our lives to Jesus in faith. What part of that picture means the most to you? What does Paul, the author of Romans, say we need to do in response to what God has done in our lives? What reason does Paul give for doing these things?

- If you could be confident that your sin and past are truly crucified and gone, what difference would that make on your life now and in the future?

- How has Jesus spoken to you in this devotional time?

## Prayer

Dear Jesus, help me to see the sin that clings to me and keeps me from living in your freedom. I confess that I have often followed my own way rather than your way. Please forgive me and help me to follow you closely. Amen.

# FEASTING INSTEAD of SNACKING

## In the Word

Read John 6:53-58 and Isaiah 55:1-2.

Have you ever heard the phrase, "Let me chew on that for a while"? Think of that metaphor as you "chew" on the words Jesus just spoke in John 6:53-58. The crowd had been focused on material needs rather than spiritual needs. They wanted physical bread and failed to recognize their hunger for spiritual sustenance. Jesus was going to have to say something drastic to break them out of their literal-mindedness so they could see their spiritual need.

The problem was the same in Isaiah's day. The people were snacking on material things rather than feasting on the richness of God's presence.

The problem can exist in our lives as well. As C.S. Lewis said in his book *The Weight of Glory:* "Our Lord finds our desire not too strong, but too weak. We are half-hearted creatures, fooling about with drink and sex and ambition when infinite joy is offered us, we are like ignorant children who want to continue making mud pies in a slum because we cannot imagine what is meant by the offer of a vacation at the sea. We are far too easily pleased."

## Eric Hellon's Story

"You need to be completely moved out by the time I get back tomorrow," said his brother over the phone. These words hit Eric hard. Almost overnight he found himself homeless, jobless, and carless.

He and his brother had been partners in business for eight years and had shared a home to keep expenses down. But now their company was being sold, leaving Eric with no job and no place to live. Plus, Eric had signed a "no-compete" clause when the company was sold so he couldn't even use his graphic and web design skills to find new clients and earn a new income.

Looking back on that time, Eric can now recognize that God was "stripping away the things I thought were so important – the cars and the clothes and all the material things. Suddenly I had nothing. All I had was God and my fiancée Taneisha. He had to strip us down so we could totally rely on Him." Even though it was hard, Eric is grateful now for the way God worked.

In the months leading up to this time, Eric had begun to get restless – there had to be something more to life. For years, Eric's whole life had revolved around his work with his brother. They built their company from the ground up, eventually having as many as twelve employees, and often working as many as sixteen hours a day. Eric first began this hectic work life when he was only fifteen , and now, at the young age of 23, he was already getting burned out from the intense pace. Something was missing.

So Eric made the decision to start attending church again. Growing up, his aunt had faithfully taken him to church, but as soon as he turned eighteen, he wanted nothing more to do with it. "I was doing things my own way, living a totally self-centered life," he admits. "Before I was saved, my life was all about money. Money was my god. So when I finally came to God, He took all that away so that I would draw close to Him."

Eric admits that his goals were so selfish that he had planned never to even get married or have kids. Ironically, Taneisha felt the same way. Neither of them had good role models of a solid marriage, so avoiding marriage seemed like a good move. But God had other plans. As God began changing both of their hearts and drawing them close to Christ, they felt led to get married. Now, almost seven years later, they look back on this and clearly see God's hand at work.

As they continued to seek Christ and put Him first in their lives and marriage, He gradually began to reshape their desires and goals. Over time they got back on their feet financially, and were eventually able to buy their own home, where they are now raising their two young children to know and love God.

When Eric looks back at where he and Taneisha have come from, he is amazed at the difference Jesus has made in their lives. "Neither of us grew up in a two-parent home. Neither of us grew up in a house that our parents owned. And now here we are, giving this future and hope to our children. We're creating a whole new legacy." And the legacy goes beyond their own little family.

Even though Eric is one of the youngest members of his extended family, many of them now come to him and his wife for advice and help. Their solid faith and strong marriage are a testimony to their family of the difference Jesus makes. God is using Eric and Taneisha to encourage other members of their family to seek Him in their own lives.

Possibly the biggest difference Jesus has made in Eric's life is a shift in his purpose. Before putting Christ at the center of his life, Eric's purpose in life was to make more money. Now, Eric says his purpose is to serve. It is that shift in focus, Eric believes, that has made his life, marriage and family strong. He seeks God's help every day to serve and love his wife and kids, and to use his gifts to serve others.

With Christ in his life, Eric says, "My life became bigger than me. It's no longer about me. It's about serving others. Like when the Bible says that as a husband, I should love my wife as Christ loved the church – that's all about serving and sacrifice."

Eric's new focus is making a difference in other areas as well. His servant attitude is quickly earning him clients in a new business venture he's started, called MamaAlwaysSays.com, that helps small businesses gain positive customer reviews. And God is using Eric to serve others with his expertise in managing money and knowledge of biblical financial principles. He's even launched a non-profit ministry called Financially Faithful to counsel others to be good stewards of their God-given resources.

It took losing everything for Eric to find Jesus. But now that he has put Jesus first, Eric has gained more than he ever imagined possible.

## Make it Personal

- In what ways are you "far too easily pleased," snacking on material junk food rather than feasting on God's presence?

- What kind of breads (material things, worries, relationships, etc.) can take your attention away from God?

- Jesus uses eating as a metaphor. What does Jesus mean when He tells us to eat Him? As you answer this question, think about what you do when you eat and what happens to food when you eat it.

- How has Jesus spoken to you in this devotional time?

## Prayer

Dear Jesus, please help me to not settle for lesser things. Help my desire for you to keep growing stronger, and help me to pursue you with all I have within me. Amen.

a spiritual practice
# FEASTING THROUGH FASTING

*"[God] humbled you by letting you hunger, then by feeding you with manna, with which neither you nor your ancestors were acquainted, in order to make you understand that one does not live by bread alone, but by every word that comes from the mouth of the Lord." Deuteronomy 8:3*

When Jesus said, "I am the bread of life," He was inviting us to find our true fulfillment in Him. He is our source of life. Yet so many things like activities, attitudes, and material items threaten to pull us away from feasting on Christ.

This is why fasting has been such an important spiritual practice in the Christian tradition. It is a time to step out of the normal rhythms of life and become more attuned to God's presence. Traditionally, fasting has served several purposes:

1.  To express repentance for sin and humble oneself before God.
2.  To surrender the desires of the flesh so that the spirit is more open to the filling of God.
3.  To devote oneself to prayer and meditation.

## STEP ONE: Consider what type of fast to engage in

Traditionally, fasting has involved abstaining from food. If you are reading this ahead of time, you may want to begin your fast after dinner on Saturday night and end your fast with a light supper on Sunday evening. If you didn't plan ahead for this, you can also simply fast from food throughout one day, or you could fast from one meal. Some people fast from everything except water, and others choose to fast from all solid food but still drink some fruit juice. Pray about which type of fast makes most sense for you.

*Note: If you have any physical conditions that would be affected by abstaining from food, please consult your doctor.*

There are other types of fasts beyond fasting from food. The intent of fasting is to help us release our attachment to anything other than God so that we can rightly enjoy God's good gifts. As Marjorie Thompson says in *Soul Feast*, "Our society voraciously consumes just about any and every thing: food, drink, sex, drugs, guns, cars, clothing, energy, gadgets, TV, computers, gossip, fads, ideologies, programs, even work and leisure."

Spend some time considering if God may be calling you to fast from something other than food today. Perhaps He is asking you to fast from shopping, media consumption, caffeine, busyness. Perhaps He is inviting you to abstain from judging others or from striving for recognition.

The question to bring to God is: What do I do to excess? We ask this question because "When what we consume is consuming us, and what we possess is possessing us, the only way back to health and balance is to refrain from using those things that have control over us" (Marjorie Thompson). By fasting from these things, we open ourselves up to allowing God more control of our lives.

## STEP TWO: Feast on God during your fast

As you surrender food or some other object or activity, shift your focus toward feasting on God instead. Ask God to help you select a focus or activity that would help you draw closer to Him. It might involve one of the following:

- Go for a walk – not for exercise, but to spend time with God.
- Listen to some worship music, and let it open your heart to God.
- Take a nap. Sometimes sleep is exactly what God is inviting you to – a time to rest your body and let Him restore you physically.
- Praise God by doing the ABC's of praise. Come up with at least one word to describe God for every letter. Turn this into a prayer.
- Write a letter of confession to God, asking Him to forgive you for whatever He reveals you need to confess.

The important thing is not to try and distract yourself from the fast. Instead, stay present to God through the day. Ask Him to reveal to you what He wants to show you through your fast. Ask God to help you recognize and honor your limits today. Perhaps you may even want to spend some time journaling how it feels to deny yourself in some way.

# Week 3

# "I Am the Light of the World"

Benjamin loved going to the Feast of Tabernacles. The festival celebrated God's presence and goodness by commemorating how God had provided for Israel during their time in the wilderness. The Feast of the Tabernacles was one of three annual Jewish festivals, but as far as Benjamin was concerned, it was by far the best.

For eight days Jerusalem partied. There were parades, music and entertainment. The goal was to try and stay up all night and then rest during the day in tents or booths. The tents were part of the festival, serving as a remembrance of the tents the Israelites lived in during their forty years in the wilderness.

Benjamin didn't spend much time in his family's tent. There was too much excitement going on. All the action was at the Temple, and it lasted all night long. There was music, dancing, singing, laughter, even rabbis juggling flaming torches. Benjamin hoped that the son of the great Rabbi Gamaliel would be there. It was said that he could juggle eight torches while dancing at the same time.

The festivities began just after sundown. That's when Benjamin would go to the Temple and join the crowds seated in the large grandstands that had been constructed for the festival. There, in the Court of Women, four very large candelabras had been hung. The lamps were so large that when they were lit, they were as bright as a full moon. And because the Temple sat at the highest point in Jerusalem, the lamps lit up the entire city.

When the sun went down, the crowd would quiet down as the Temple musicians solemnly paraded in and took their places on the steps. The priests then entered in and took their places. Finally, a group of teenagers, the sons of priests, marched in carrying large containers of oil. Benjamin stood on tiptoe to watch as they climbed ladders and began pouring gallons of oil into the bowls of the candelabras. The priests then began the ritual pronouncements, followed by singing. Then at the climatic moment, there was a trumpet blast and the candelabras were lit.

Benjamin had been taught by his parents that the lamp lighting celebrated God's presence, as they remembered how God was with them as a pillar of fire during the Exodus, and by looking forward in hope that the Messiah would come soon to lead them out of their bondage to Rome.

It was a stirring moment as the light of the lamps grew to a dazzling brightness. Some cheered while others stood in silent wonder. Some brushed away tears as the flame light danced in their eyes. Then it happened – a man shouted out, "I am the Light of the World!"

# BLINDED

## In the Word

Read John 8:12-32, John 9:39-41 and 2 Corinthians 4:4-6.

The debate between Jesus and the Pharisees is filled with irony. When Jesus proclaimed that He was the Light of the World, this meant He was the fulfillment of everything the lamp lighting ceremony stood for. *(Read the introduction to Week Three to learn more about this ceremony.)* But the Pharisees refused to see. Because they rejected Jesus, they were blind to the truth.

That still happens today. We have a deep need for true direction in life. But without Jesus, we are blind to what makes life truly satisfying and fulfilling. This happens in big ways, as you will see in the story below, but it can also happen in small ways. Whenever we turn a blind eye to any part of God's instructions, we blind ourselves to the full presence of the Light of the World.

## Dennis Pinney's Story

Dennis had his first beer at the age of seven, and things went downhill from there. By the time he was eighteen, Dennis had dropped out of college and joined a band. He thought life couldn't get any better. He had a job where it was okay to spend his days boozing, getting high, and chasing women. And that's exactly how Dennis spent the next twenty-plus years of his life. He traveled with bands and spent his days stoned, drunk or both.

But after twenty years, his habits had just about destroyed his life. He ended up living out of a van, with only a couple pairs of jeans, a few t-shirts, his guitar and an amp, all because buying drugs seemed more important than paying his bills. He looked terrible, with an unkempt beard and long scraggly hair. He was dirty more often than he was clean.

Every so often, Dennis would have moments of clarity where he would think to himself, "This is not who I wanted to be." But he saw no way out. He couldn't imagine life without alcohol and drugs. He had convinced himself that a life without those things would be boring. He'd rather die than live like that. During these "moments of clarity," Dennis thought about ending it all, but instead, he'd get high again.

Dennis had a stepfather who tried to help by talking to Dennis about things like character, integrity, courage, responsibility, and having purpose. But Dennis didn't listen. In fact, Dennis admits that at the time, he couldn't even understand what his stepfather was talking about. Those character traits were so foreign to Dennis that they made no sense to him at all. In Dennis' view, his stepfather was trying to turn him into a boring person.

The turning point came when Dennis' wife moved out. She was tired of living out of a van. Dennis dealt with this by drinking four bottles of Schnapps, smoking a lot of marijuana, and then going to see the pastor who had married them. The plan in his foggy mind was to have the pastor tell his wife that she needed to do whatever Dennis wanted. Dennis thought that was in the Bible somewhere.

The pastor invited Dennis into his home and Dennis vaguely recalls the pastor talking to him before everything seemed to fade away from his consciousness. He still struggles to put words to what he experienced next. He felt surrounded by warmth and a bright light. "It was sort of like being enveloped in a cloud," he says, but admits this doesn't adequately describe his experience.

Then Dennis heard a clear voice speaking to him. "Are you done with this?" the voice asked. "If you will accept my Son as your foundation and Savior, I will relieve you of all this."

"Yes, I'll accept," Dennis remembers thinking. And then the experience was over and he heard the pastor saying, "Dennis, do you want to pray the sinner's prayer?"

Dennis did pray that prayer and then got back into his van, wondering what had just happened. That was not like any drug-induced high he had ever experienced. In that moment, Dennis made a decision. He pulled over to the side of the road and started dumping out all of his alcohol, drugs and drug paraphernalia. He didn't stop until everything was gone. He was really glad the police didn't drive by while he was dumping everything out into the ditch on the side of the road.

That night Dennis put his head on his pillow and fell asleep. It was evidence of God's presence because he should have been too high on stimulants to sleep. Dennis thinks this was probably the first time in twenty years that he actually fell asleep naturally instead of passing out.

The next morning he told a friend he was through with drugs. His friend's response was, "If that's the case, why not smoke one last farewell joint before you quit." Dennis thought this was a great idea, but after taking his first hit, he again heard a voice say, "Dennis, I told you I would relieve you of this." That jarred him. He handed the joint back and walked away.

Dennis never returned to drugs. God miraculously took away his desire.

The next miracle followed quickly. Dennis didn't have a job and he had few job skills outside of guitar playing. So he signed up for a state sponsored job training program and took some tests to determine what his vocational aptitudes might be.

When the counselor met with him to go over the scores, he said, "In all my years on this job, I've never seen anything like this." Even though Dennis had dropped out of college and had spent twenty years stoned and drunk, his scores were so high they were off the charts. Because he scored so well, Dennis was sent to college to study computer science. Today, he is a computer network specialist.

The only similarity between who the old Dennis was and the man he is today is his guitar playing. Dennis once used his musical ability to worship a destructive lifestyle, but now he's thrilled he can use that gift to worship God as he plays for his church.

Dennis has also remarried, but this time it's a healthy marriage, the kind he never would have dreamed possible, the kind he thought would be boring.

"I've become the man my stepfather used to try to tell me about – a man of integrity, courage, responsibility, and purpose – a man of character," he smiles. "I wasted so many years thinking this life would be boring. I can't believe how wrong I was."

As Dennis looks back at how far he's come, he marvels at the greatness and goodness of God. He can't believe all the ways God has worked in his life. "When I first became a Christian, if I had written a list of all the things I wanted to become," he says, "it wouldn't have touched what God has actually done. My life far surpasses anything I could have dreamt of back then."

*Do you want to pray the "Sinner's Prayer" asking Jesus to come into your life? You can find it on page 219.*

## Make it Personal

- In 2 Corinthians 4:4, it says that the "god of this age" has blinded people to the truth of who Jesus is – a blindness Dennis experienced for many years. In what ways have you been blinded?

- How might God be shining a light into any dark places in your life today?

- In John 8:31-32, what does Jesus say will allow us to know the truth and be set free by it?

- In what areas of your life might you be turning a blind eye to some of God's instructions? Ask God to help you reflect on this, and then confess any places in your life where you're not following His directions for you.

- How has Jesus spoken to you in this devotional time?

## Prayer

Dear Jesus, please remove any blinders in my life, any places where I am not walking in your light. Help me to know your truth and allow you to set me free by your truth today. Amen.

# INTO the LIGHT

## In the Word

Read John 8:12 and John 1:4-5.

Depression, failure, heartbreak—these are things that can darken our lives. But in the midst of our darkness, Jesus declares "I am the light of the world."

His presence brings:

- hope where there is despair
- courage where there is fear
- acceptance where there is rejection
- healing where there is pain
- freedom where there is bondage
- forgiveness where there is condemnation
- new life where there is no life

Light always conquers darkness – ALWAYS – but only if we choose to uncover it.

## Paul Pom's Story

Paul's life was crashing down around him. His wife of 17 years had announced that their marriage was no longer working and she wanted out. Paul was crushed. What went wrong?

One day, while driving, he went over everything that might have gone wrong. In particular, he thought about his obsession with horror. Paul loved horror films, haunted houses and the creepy, scary, darker side of things.

For Paul, Halloween was like Christmas. He even used his craftsman skills to create scary special effects for a haunted house every year and got so good at it that he started doing it professionally. But his obsession dominated his time and thoughts. Instead of spending time with his family, he always seemed to be working on the next horror project.

As Paul drove, he wondered how he got so deeply involved in horror. When did it begin? Then he remembered that "it was after my mom left us when I was seven. I figured that if I surrounded myself with enough scary monsters, I'd be protected." It's exactly how a seven-year-old would think.

It might have been a coincidence, but as soon as he made the connection between his mom leaving and his obsession with horror, his hands started to tingle and then went numb. The numbness continued up his arms. "By the time I was able to pull off the road, my whole upper body was tingling," Paul shares.

He didn't know what was going on. He looked up into the sky and said, "Are you doing this?" Anyone who knew Paul back then would be surprised to hear him ask this. He wasn't the kind of guy to give God much thought. However, he had recently started attending church on occasion. So, maybe God was on Paul's mind a little more than He used to be.

After a few minutes, everything went back to normal, and Paul was able to get back on the road again. That's when his daughter sent him a text message. He knew it was unsafe to take his eyes off the road, but Paul looked down at the message – a little longer than he realized – and when he looked up he saw that he was only a few feet from the end of the road.

Paul slammed on his brakes and the car skidded towards the dead end until it finally screeched to a stop. When Paul looked up, all he saw was a big yellow sign a few inches from the front of his car that said "END."

For Paul, this was a sign from God (literally) that his old life was coming to an end. He instinctively knew that God wanted him to stop focusing on horror and start focusing on Him. Soon after that experience, Paul surrendered his life to Jesus' control. He candidly admits, however, that "I did it more in hope that Jesus could offer me relief from my pain, rather than out of a desire for a relationship with Him."

Seeking guidance, Paul met with the pastor of his church who recommended to Paul that he get involved in a men's group. That group of men became Paul's lifeline. Week after week he came to the group and unloaded his frustrations, struggles and sorrows. Paul felt like a sponge who filled up with junk all week and then was able to wring it all out at the group meeting. The other men in the group let Paul share his pain. As they listened with patience and support, Paul began to experience relief.

At church and in his group, Paul kept hearing about the relationship Jesus wanted to have with him. He also saw this relationship modeled by the guys in his group. With their help, he began to build his own relationship with Jesus.

Paul also began to learn how to pray. The only prayer Paul knew was the Lord's Prayer, and after his wife left him, he started praying that prayer every night. That wasn't a bad place to start, but through the example of the guys in his group, Paul began to learn that prayer was simply a conversation with God.

Through his men's group, Paul also learned how to study his Bible. He especially gravitated toward verses that referred to light conquering the darkness. As Paul nourished his relationship with Jesus, he began to be transformed. He no longer spent his days thinking about the next scary project he could build. Instead, he found himself thinking about Jesus.

Paul put into practice what the Bible teaches in Philippians 4:8: "Finally, brothers and sisters, whatever is true, whatever is noble, whatever is right, whatever is pure, whatever is lovely, whatever is admirable – if anything is excellent or praiseworthy – think about such things."

Then Paul had another God moment. He remembers it clearly. One morning he woke up and felt different. "It felt like being a kid without a care in the world." That was a big change for a man who had felt crushed by emotional pain. This was a turning point for Paul. He had reached a point where he knew Jesus was with him, and his trust in Jesus was setting him free from his pain.

Jesus is completely real to Paul now. He has learned how to go to Jesus and "wring out the sponge" in prayer each day. And it's made a difference. Now, when he faces a challenge or feels stress building, he quickly goes to God in prayer. He knows he has an anchor in the storm that he can count on. And the darkness is gone. Paul now spends his creative energies sharing God's light, and he loves it.

## Make it Personal

- What types of darkness have you experienced in your life? Where have you looked for light?

- In John 8:12, what does Jesus say we must do to experience His light?

- Sometimes, when people are depressed, they pull away from church and fellowship groups. Why would they do that? In what way is that counter-productive? How could church, or a fellowship group like the one Paul talked about, help you experience the light?

- How has Jesus spoken to you in this devotional time?

## Prayer

Dear Jesus, please reveal any places of darkness in my life – any dark thoughts, emotions, habits, or sins that need to be surrendered to you. Help me to step into your light today and shine brightly for you. Amen.

# BLINDED by RULES

## In the Word

Read John 9.

In John 9, you read a story of a man who was born blind, but step-by-step he not only gained his physical sight, but his spiritual sight as well. On the other hand, the Pharisees, who had physical sight, step-by-step showed that they were spiritually blind.

The sticking point for the Pharisees seems to be that Jesus performed His healing on a Sabbath, and healing on the Sabbath broke one of the Pharisees' rules. You need to understand that there was no biblical command against healing on the Sabbath. The rule was man-made. It was an attempt to precisely define the biblical command about not working on the Sabbath.

For the Pharisees, keeping the rules was a measure of whether or not a person was godly. In their misguided thinking, Jesus could not be the Messiah because He was a rule breaker. In the Pharisees' attempt to follow God, they ended up making rules that blinded them to the truth.

Is it possible, however good our intentions, that we do the same thing?

## Tammy & Dan Smith's Story

Tammy grew up knowing absolutely nothing about God. So, when her boyfriend (now her husband), Dan, asked her to watch some videos with him about creation versus evolution, she thought it was a waste of time. She said, "I knew God didn't exist and Christianity was just a crutch for needy people." However, she liked spending time with Dan and figured watching videos wouldn't be so bad if it meant spending more time with him. Besides, she was college educated. She wasn't going to get duped.

By the time they finished watching the videos, Tammy was scared. "Oh no," she thought, "there might really be a Creator."

Dan then invited Tammy to come to a Bible study with him. Her response was: "A Bible study? Are you crazy! And on Friday nights!"

She must have *really* liked Dan, because she ended up going, but she hated it. She thought the people at the study were weird. They talked differently, acted differently, and had different values. They weren't normal. What normal person would spend a Friday night studying a relic like the Bible? But she kept coming back every week.

After three months, Tammy's attitude began to shift. Tammy realized that she was starting to look forward to Bible study every Friday. The people no longer seemed weird. Instead, they intrigued her. They were caring, committed, and fun to be with. And they never seemed bothered by her lack of knowledge. She started to like the differences she saw in them.

Looking back, she can't pinpoint an exact moment that it happened, but she knows that she began that Bible study not caring about Jesus, and came out as a believer who was in love with Jesus.

Everything about Jesus was new and exciting to Tammy. It was the same for Dan, who was just returning to faith in Jesus himself. They were soaking everything in like sponges and wanted to talk about Jesus all of the time.

They were passionate about glorifying God, but being new, they didn't always know how to do it in mature, healthy ways. They started falling into the trap of a rule-bound faith. In their mind, television was bad. Secular music was bad. Not talking about Jesus all of the time was bad. Everything, it seemed, was bad.

"I felt guilty any time I did these 'bad things,'" Tammy says. "and I resented it." Their new Christian life became increasingly rigid and rule-driven. They found it increasingly difficult to live up to all the expectations they had piled on themselves. When they looked around and noticed that other Christians weren't trying to live up to the standards they thought were so important, Tammy and Dan became bitter. As they saw it, these Christians weren't trying to be any different than non-Christians.

At first, Tammy and Dan felt superior to others, then judgmental, and finally resentful. "We developed ugly hearts," Tammy recalls. "We didn't love the people Jesus died for."

They were excited when Dan got a job opportunity that would move them out of town. By now, they couldn't stand Christians. None of them measured up in their eyes. They were also ready to be done with Jesus. The Christian life (or their rule-bound, graceless, unloving version of it) was just too hard. Ironically, all the rules they created for Christian living caused them to walk away from Jesus.

Moving gave them the opportunity to make a clean break. Tammy and Dan didn't go back to church or make Christian friends for ten years, and their kids were growing up not knowing anything about God. But then Tammy and Dan came to a point where they realized, "We need to get back to Jesus." The realization seemed to come out of nowhere. It wasn't something they had been thinking about for awhile. There had been no event that occurred that changed their minds. They literally woke up one morning with the thought, "We need to get back to Jesus."

Knowing that it was going to be very difficult to make changes in the environment they were in, they decided to move again. Within a week Dan had a new job and their house was up for sale.

Once they moved, they started looking for a church and soon found a warm, friendly, grace-filled church where they could start getting reconnected to Jesus. "Now life is completely different," Tammy says, "We're once again passionate about glorifying God and growing in our relationship with Him, but this time we are doing it without all the rules and judgment."

Tammy and Dan have been discovering God's secret ingredient to life. It's called grace. It's made their lives so much better. The bitterness, disillusionment, and resentfulness they once felt have been lifted and replaced with joy and love for others.

The funny thing is that they have returned to doing some of the same practices that used to feel so burdensome to them before, only this time it feels different. They are no longer doing these things in order to keep some kind of rule. Now they realize it's a choice they make. And because it's a choice, it doesn't feel like a burden. They also don't expect or demand that other Christians make the same choices.

They're discovering that there is a lot of choice in picking practices that can help them best experience the presence of Jesus. The practices that work for them may be different from the things that are helpful to others. This freedom of choice has made living for God fun and exciting again – and filled with grace.

## Make it Personal

- Have you or someone you know ever lived a rule-bound faith? What did that look like? How did that rule-bound faith affect others who observed it?

- In what ways were the Pharisees in John 9 blinded by the rules?

- What rules, if any, might Jesus still want us to live by? How might this fit with the concept of grace that Tammy and Dan are discovering?

- If you struggle with being judgmental or rule-bound in your faith, ask Jesus to help remove the burden of legalism and replace it with His grace.

- How has Jesus spoken to you in this devotional time?

## Prayer

Dear Jesus, I know there is no way I could ever possibly keep all the laws of God perfectly. That's why I need you to be my Savior. Please help me walk in the freedom of your grace today, allowing you to transform me from the inside-out with your love. Amen.

# MISSING PIECES

## In the Word

Read Psalm 139.

Jesus, the "light of the world," can shine His light into the deepest, darkest recesses of our souls. He knows things about us that we do not even know ourselves. He knows where we need to grow and where we need to heal. He knows the holes in our lives that need to be filled. He knows our greatest desires and our deepest needs – needs we can sense but can't quite identify, desires that create longings that are too deeply buried to identify. Jesus is our Light. And as we trust Him, He will guide us in ways that will meet our deepest needs and satisfy our strongest desires.

## Sandi Padilla's Story

A piece of her heart was missing – until the day she met her birth mom.

Sandi was fortunate. She had been raised in a loving, Christian home, with parents who lived out what they believed. They were patient, kind, generous, and self-sacrificing. And their example made it easy for Sandi to know and follow Christ from an early age. But something was still missing.

She knew she had been adopted, and she was truly thankful for the parents God had given her. But she couldn't help wondering about her birth mother. Some adoptees struggle with issues of abandonment, but from an early age, Sandi was comforted by the words of Psalm 139:13 that say, "… you knit me together in my mother's womb." These words gave Sandi a deep sense of security, knowing that God was sovereign over every detail of her life.

At the age of eleven, Sandi began to pray for her birth mother. "I kept wondering who this woman was who had an unexpected event happen in her life and who wanted me to have a whole, complete family," says Sandi. "Who was this woman who sacrificially gave me the gift of my family?" Sandi also wanted to be sure her birth mother knew that she didn't hold any anger or bitterness toward her. And she especially wanted to find out if her mother had a relationship with Jesus.

Finally, in her twenties, Sandi worked up the courage to look for her birth mother. Sandi eventually discovered that her records were held in an office in Sacramento, and after receiving permission to view them, the social worker told Sandi there was something unusual in the file – a letter.

Her birth mother had written her a letter, trusting that one day she would receive it. Sandi cried as she read her mother's words of love and care for Sandi, and the story of her personal Christian testimony. Sandi read that when her birth mother was pregnant with her, she had walked away from Christ. After the pregnancy, she began searching different religions. But eventually she discovered that truth is only found in Jesus Christ. So she came back to Jesus, and He flooded her life with His light, love and forgiveness.

God used that letter to bring some healing into Sandi's heart that day, and "to put together some of the missing pieces of my life," she says. Then Sandi smiles and says, "My family grew – literally overnight – and I saw what a wonderful Christian heritage I had been given." She and her birth mother had a beautiful reunion shortly after that, and their relationship has continued to grow over the past 25 years.

Sandi also briefly met her birth father many years ago, but didn't really have any interaction with him until just a few weeks ago when she learned that he was in a hospital, near death. Sandi and her husband, Steve, recognized that this might be her last opportunity to have any real connection with him. So they jumped on a plane and headed to Las Vegas.

While they were there, they ended up staying in a hotel shaped like a pyramid. It became apparent to Sandi that God had set this up, because He used that hotel to speak to her. As she looked at the Egyptian artwork and landscaping of this hotel, she began to see that God was freeing her from her own personal Egypt. "I didn't realize that I had been enslaved by fear and insecurity," says Sandi. "I felt like an illegitimate daughter, at least from my father's side."

As she walked out of the hotel, she was reminded of Moses and how God had a plan for his life. God protected him and allowed him to be found in that basket in the water and adopted into Pharaoh's family. Sandi says that in that moment, "God spoke to me and said, 'I've redeemed you out of Egypt, out of fear, out of insecurity. You are my daughter and I love you.'" She could feel the love of God wash over her.

This experience with God prepared her to meet her birth father, from whom she had always felt disconnected. The time they were able to spend together brought an even deeper healing and restoration to Sandi's heart, and she could see how God was using her in her father's life as well.

Sandi has walked with Christ for most of her life, and God has used both her birth parents and adopted parents to help her know more about how much He loves her. "I can see how God planned my life and orchestrated all the events of my life," she shares.

This thought reminds Sandi of her life verse from Psalm 37:4 where it says, "Delight yourself in the Lord and he will give you the desires of your heart." Reflecting on this verse, Sandi says, "It really was part of His plan for me to know my birth mother AND my birth father. I had no idea how important these pieces in my life were and how they looked in the tapestry God is weaving in my life. And it's a beautiful picture."

## Make it Personal

- In Psalm 139, it says there is nowhere you can go to flee from God – He is everywhere. Even though this is true, have there been times when you have tried to flee from God? What happened? How did God draw you back – or how might He be drawing you back now?

- In Psalm 139:11-12, the Psalmist says that even darkness is not dark to God – His light shines through any darkness. Where in your life have you seen His light shine? Has He brought to light any needs or desires within you that He wants to meet?

- In Psalm 139:23-24, the Psalmist asks God to search his heart and reveal anything that might pull him away from God. Has God brought to light any areas of sin in your life that He wants you to confess and be forgiven for? Take time to talk with Him about this.

- As you consider the events of your life, perhaps like Sandi, you feel there are still some missing pieces or things that don't make sense. Ask God to fill your heart and mind with His light and help you to trust Him with those unanswered questions in your life.

- How has Jesus spoken to you in this devotional time?

## Prayer

Dear Jesus, thank you that you have searched me and known me. You know me better than I know myself. Help me to trust that even if I don't understand you, I can trust you. Even if I don't know what the future holds, you do know, and you have good plans for my life. Thank you! Amen.

# EXPOSURE

## In the Word

Read Genesis 1:26-27, John 8:32, and 1 John 1:5-9.

Jesus, "the light of the world," exposes the darkness in our lives. He sees what is ugly in us, but also what is magnificent about us. Jesus can see in us the image of God we are created in and He wants to shine His light in our lives so that we can see it as well.

It can be hard to see the image of God in our lives. It gets buried under years of rejections, failures, and sins – sins done by us and sins done to us. That's why we need the Light of the World. We need to see the magnificent truth about who we really are in God's eyes.

But before the magnificent truth can shine from our lives, we need to face the ugly truth. We need to expose our dark secrets of sin to the Light of the World. We do this by admitting the truth about our sins and renouncing them as wrong. When we expose the darkness, it gets obliterated by God's brilliant light. Then we can live free. We are no longer afraid of the dark things inside of us because they have been replaced by the Light!

## Dee Bright's Story

Years ago while digging up an old dying rosebush, Dee discovered how rotten the bush's roots had become. "They were twined and gnarled around each other," she recalls, "and covered with a disgusting, black slime." At the time she had no idea that years later, God would use this experience to paint a picture of a dark secret she was keeping.

This secret began at an early age.

From the time she was quite young, Dee found a unique way to escape from the pain in her life. By retreating into her mind, she discovered she could find comfort and love through fantasizing. As a young girl, she would often replay and develop the romantic stories from books she read or shows she watched. As she got older, she started to create her own fantasies.

In these mental escapes, she became the beautiful, cherished woman who was pursued by a man – often a real man she desired. Although many women have found this type of escape through reading romance novels, Dee's imagination was so well developed that she could create these stories in her own head. This escape soon turned into an addiction.

By escaping into her mind, Dee says, "I was able to tune out the feelings of abandonment I experienced as a result of growing up without my biological father, who died before I was born. Later, it also helped me cope with feelings of rejection I felt from my stepfather." Dee doesn't ever remember her stepfather smiling at her, taking her hand, or even telling her that he loved her. In fact, Dee remembers that "he was very callous toward me. He picked on me incessantly. He made me feel stupid and undesirable."

Although her mental escape provided some relief, her fantasies began to take over her waking life. Even when she was surrounded by people, she could still find herself zoning out and retreating into a fantasy.

Relief finally came when Dee married the man she thought she would spend the rest of her life with. During this time, she didn't feel the need to escape into her fantasy world and was able to stay focused on living her real life. But the reality of an increasingly painful marriage eventually became too much to bear. She did all she could to make her marriage work, but after ten years of unsuccessful effort, her marriage ended.

Dee soon returned to her "coping mechanism," as she calls it. "First I got really mad at God," she says, "and then I got really stupid." Once again finding herself alone and feeling unwanted, Dee began to weave stories in her mind to escape the pain.

She also began looking elsewhere for relief, becoming involved in several affairs with married men. She was still looking for the love and validation she had always longed for, but her behavior only added to her guilt and shame.

On the surface, Dee was able to hide her sins. No one would have guessed that she was living this double life. Inside she knew the truth, but didn't know how to break free. But God did.

He led Dee to a small group Bible study where she began to experience God's love through the members. Next, she began sensing God telling her it was time to confide her sin to a trusted Christian friend. "I balked. It was one of the hardest things I've ever had to do," she says. "But I knew that to begin to get free of my sin, I needed to say it out loud. God was prompting me to expose the darkness to the light."

With fear in her heart, she went for a walk with one of her closest friends and began sharing her story. "My friend listened without saying anything. Finally, after a long, scary silence, she told me she had actually struggled with some very similar things!"

That was only the beginning. With her sin brought to light, God began to lead Dee on the path toward wholeness. During the process, God ripped off Dee's blinders and gave her the powerful visual image of that dying rosebush. Through His eyes she could see slimy black roots entangled in and through her heart, infesting her life and keeping her in bondage.

She cried out to God to forgive her, and in desperation, she pleaded with Him, "Please! Rip it out!" At that moment, Dee envisioned God's light shining into those dark places, tearing out and destroying the repulsive, decaying roots that had a hold on her heart.

Dee knows she could never have been set free without God's help. It took a long time and included godly counseling, copious reading, Bible study, support from her pastor and a few close Christian friends, and mostly, "clinging to Jesus for dear life."

"It was a painful process," Dee shares. "But when God ripped out that ugliness, He then poured His warm, loving Self into those wounded, hurting places. In fact, I wear a ring to remind of me what He did for me. Now I can't imagine ever being without Him. From that point on," says Dee, "it was—and is—just a process of letting God point out those dark places and allowing Him to expose them to the light."

One of Dee's favorite scriptures that encouraged her on this journey is

Psalm 119:105, where it says, "Your word is a lamp to my feet and a light for my path." She says it's a good reminder that God only reveals a few steps at a time as we walk with Him.

Dee admits that "There are moments I feel lonely and wish I had someone in my life. But when I see what God does for me and how complete His love is, I realize no man can love me that deeply or fully. Spending time with Him, listening to Him, understanding how He sees me – He's wooing me, pursuing me. Only God can love me that way." Dee says that she is wide open for God to bring a man into her life. But if that happens, "it'll be the icing on the cake – only God can be my actual cake!"

## Make it Personal

- What does it mean to you that you are made in the image of God? How does this knowledge change the way you see yourself? The way you see others? How do you think Jesus sees you today?

- According to I John 1:7, what happens to our relationships with when we are walking in the light?

- Both John 8:32 and I John 1:6 talk about truth. What is the connection between truth and Jesus, the Light of the World?

- It can be painful to bring our sin into the light. Read I John 1:5-9 again and consider: What sin might you secretly be holding onto that Jesus wants you to reveal to the light? It may be something you are able to successfully hide from others, but Jesus sees your heart. Why not follow Dee's example and ask God to "rip it out!"

- How has Jesus spoken to you in this devotional time?

## Prayer

Dear Jesus, please shine your light on me today so that I can see the truth about myself – both the dark areas of sin, and the beautiful ways in which you created me in your image. Help me to live in your light today, Lord Jesus. Amen.

# Day 20

# WIDE-EYED

## In the Word

Read John 9 again. As you read, pay attention to the dawning realization of the blind man regarding who Jesus was.

This miracle, as real as it was, can also serve as a metaphor for our dawning awareness of who Jesus is and the difference He can make in our lives. Because of his healing, the blind man was open to seeing Jesus. The Pharisees, however, closed their eyes to the miracle and to Jesus, and they became blind.

If we are willing to at least be open to the possibility of Jesus' presence, and to the possibility that He can make a difference in our lives, we will begin to see His light shine in our darkness. The more open we are, the more we will see and experience.

## Jaime Weddell's Story

Jaime is counting her blessings. She's married to a terrific husband, with two great kids. "But when I think about what my life could have been like," she says, "I can't help but see signs of Jesus at work in my life, even when I refused to believe in Him."

As a teenager, Jaime attended church with her stepmom, primarily because she was interested in a cute boy there. But Jaime rejected everything she heard at church. "I had plenty of friends who said they were Christians," Jaime remembers, "but they lived no differently than I did. I knew my life certainly didn't match up with what the church taught." This only reinforced Jaime's belief that Christianity was a sham and that if Jesus ever did exist, He was dead now.

Jaime's resistance to Christianity was further strengthened when her dad was diagnosed with stage four brain cancer. Over the next several months, Jaime watched her dad deteriorate and suffer. Shortly before Jaime's eighteenth birthday, her father committed his life to Jesus and died soon after that.

He died knowing he could count on eternal life, but as far as Jaime was concerned, her dad was crazy. She dismissed his decision to believe in Jesus as a result of the cancer scrambling his mind. "I was certain there was no God," she says. "And even if there was a God, I didn't want to know Him because He had taken my father away."

After her dad's death, Jaime became angry and rebellious. She decided her life was going to be all about her. She would only feel secure if she was in control. "If I had continued down that path, who knows what my life would be like now," she reflects. "It would have been messy."

But something unexpected happened shortly after her dad died. Jaime met a guy. "Eli was a Christian," she says, "but he was different from any guy I had ever known, including the so-called 'Christian' guys." The other guys Jaime had known were only after one thing, but not him. Eli actually wanted to have a genuine friendship with her. And she found it rather strange.

He was interested in her as a person. He liked hanging out with her, and he liked her for who she was, without being judgmental. That was very different. Eli even introduced her to his family and invited her to church.

At first, Jaime didn't want to have a "dating relationship" with him. "That would be crazy, since I didn't believe in God," she says. But just the same, she loved hanging out with Eli. So that's what they did – they hung out, but didn't "date." Eventually, his friendship finally won her over. She fell in love and they became husband and wife.

Even though Jaime was in love with her husband, she still didn't believe in Jesus. At that time, Eli had to work on Sundays, so she had a reason not to go to church. But her husband was starting to change her mind about Christianity.

"Eli had a real faith in Jesus," she explains, "and it made a noticeable difference in the way he lived his life." Compared to all the phonies Jaime had known, she noticed a consistent godly character in Eli, and it was softening her heart towards God.

While Jaime was pregnant with their first child, she decided it was time to try church again. "There's something about preparing to be a parent that gets you thinking more seriously about faith," she says. At that same time, Eli's schedule changed so that he no longer had to work on Sundays. So they started attending church together.

For the next six months, Jaime went to church, and she watched, listened, and learned about having a relationship with Jesus. But she wasn't ready to make a commitment. Then one Sunday it all seemed to click. When the pastor gave an "altar call" at the end of the service that week, Jaime, heavy with child, nearly ran to the front. "That's when I prayed to commit my life to Jesus and become a Christian," she says. That was four years ago and Jaime has never once regretted her decision.

That also began a time of growth for Jaime and Eli. He had a heart for working with teens, so shortly after she made her decision to follow Jesus, they began volunteering to work with the youth group at church. Eli would take the lead, and Jaime would learn more about Jesus and the Bible right along with the youth.

Since then she has experienced Jesus' presence in countless ways. "I can't even begin to count the times when our finances were low and we didn't know how we were going to pay the next bill," she says, "and the money would unexpectedly show up through a surprise bonus, a side job, or a gift from a generous friend."

These experiences are helping Jaime learn more about the loving character of God. In addition, Jamie says, "Now I feel secure. I used to think I could only be secure by being in control, but that didn't work. I could never be in complete control. Now I know that God is in control, and I've learned from experience that I can count on God."

She also sees Jesus' presence through the love of her husband and precious kids. She remembers before she was a Christian hearing a preacher say that husbands should love God more than their wives. She thought that was ludicrous. "I want a husband who loves me more than anything—including God," she thought. But now she understands. She has a husband who loves God even more than he loves her, and she realizes that because he loves God more, he is able to love her better.

Jaime has a marriage and family she never imagined possible. When she thinks of what might have been if she had stayed on her angry, rebellious, God-rejecting course, she gives God thanks. She can see the difference Jesus has made.

## Make it Personal

- Just like the blind man in John 9, and Jaime in today's story, our faith journey often involves a whole series of events and circumstances that draw us to God. Where are you on the journey today? Still seeking and asking questions? Recognizing that Jesus is real and ready to make a commitment? Following Christ and growing in Him? Wandering away and needing to come back?

- Sometimes we don't notice God reaching out to us until we look back at it later. Take a moment and reflect: What events, scriptures, etc., has God used in the past to draw you toward Jesus? How might He be trying to get your attention now? If you are ready to make a decision to follow Jesus, there is a prayer you can use on page 219.

- When questioned about Jesus, the blind man answers that although he doesn't know exactly who Jesus is, he does know that he once was blind but now he sees. Even though, like the blind man, you might not be able to explain everything about Jesus, what experiences have you had of Him that you could share with others?

- How has Jesus spoken to you in this devotional time?

## Prayer

Dear Jesus, you are truly the Light of the World. Open my eyes to see the ways you are working in and around me, and like the blind man, help me to share you with others. Amen.

a spiritual practice
# PRAYER of EXAMEN

One way we can become more aware of Jesus' light in our life is through the prayer of Examen. The prayer of Examen is an ancient spiritual practice that involves discerning the movements of God in our daily life. The Examen is often done in the evening for ten to fifteen minutes, and can become an excellent way to connect with God at the end of the day. Take time to pray backward through the events of the past 24 hours using the following guide:

1. **BE STILL**
   *"Be still and know that I am God..."* *(Psalm 46:10)*
   Take a few moments to relax, let go and focus your attention on the presence of God.

2. **ASK FOR DISCERNMENT**
   *"Send out your light and your truth; let them lead me..."* *(Psalm 43:3)*
   Ask the Holy Spirit to help you discern God's movement in and around you today.

3. **REMEMBER & GIVE THANKS**
   *"Bless the Lord, O my soul, and do not forget all his benefits"* *(Ps. 103)*
   Spend some time remembering with gratitude a few of the specific gifts of this day: gifts of existence, work, relationships, and place; gifts of challenge, growth and conflict; a meeting with a friend, a moment of insight, a glimpse of natural beauty, a considerate driver. Savor the memory and offer thanks for every gift encountered.

4. **REFLECT & LISTEN**
   *"Search me, O God, and know my heart..."* *(Psalm 139)*

Reflect on what has been happening to you today, trusting that the Spirit will reveal what needs to come to light. What particular moments do you "see" in your mind's eye as you replay this time? What feelings, positive and negative, did these experiences evoke in you? Listen to these feelings without judgment or even interpretation. If you feel bewildered or puzzled, ask yourself if there might be something new unfolding in your experience, and pray once more for illumination and clarity, trusting God to reveal this to you.

## 5. RESPOND TO GOD

*"Have mercy on me, O God, according to your steadfast love" (Ps. 51)*
Having reviewed your past day, look upon yourself with compassion and see your need for God. Try to realize and receive God's love for you. Express sorrow for sin and especially ask forgiveness for the times that you resisted God today. Give thanks for grace and the presence of God. Especially praise God for the times you responded in ways that allowed you to draw closer to Him and see Him more clearly.

## 6. LOOK FORWARD WITH HOPE

*"When I awake I shall be satisfied, beholding your likeness…" (Ps. 17)*
Look forward in hope to tomorrow. Pray for the sensitivity to recognize God in whatever way He may choose to come to you tomorrow.

**Prayer of Examen with Your Family** *"God Sightings"*
This simplified version can be a great exercise to try with your family. At the dinner table each night, ask these simple questions and give everyone a chance to answer.

- *What was your high point today?*
- *What was your low point today? How did you see God in this?*

This is a great opportunity to share with one another what has happened in your day. This can also be a time of looking for "God Sightings" in each person's life. If someone had a difficult day, this can be a time to express care for one another, as well as to celebrate the positive experiences as gifts from God. This simple exercise will help heighten your family's awareness of God's presence and activity in their lives on a daily basis.

# Week 4

# "I Am the Good Shepherd"

The growl snapped him to full attention. He gripped his club and moved to a crouch, ready to jump into action. Behind him he could hear an uneasy stirring. He peered out into the darkness, trying to see past the firelight. The fire was a two-edged sword. It provided needed warmth for the long cold night and it usually served as a deterrent that kept predators away. But on nights when a predator was especially determined, the fire became a liability, diminishing your field of view and giving you very little reaction time.

This predator, a wolf based on the type of growl, must be especially hungry to ignore the fire and be willing to risk a battle with a shepherd. But to a wolf with a painfully empty stomach and the smell of sheep in its nostrils, the risk was worth it.

The shepherd tensed for battle, listening for any sound that might give him a moment's warning. He knew this could be a life or death fight. If he had just been a hired hand, he would have run away. No wage was worth risking your life. But he was not a hired hand. The sheep behind him were his own. He had watched them be born and given each of them their names. He would never leave them unprotected.

Then, like a black shadow, the wolf came leaping into the ring of firelight. The yellow flash of light that reflected off the back of the wolf's eye was the shepherd's only warning. In one bound, the wolf was flying towards the shepherd's throat with mouth wide open and teeth ready to clamp down on the soft flesh.

But as quick as the wolf was, the shepherd was just as quick. Timing his swing perfectly, he hit the wolf on the side of the head with the heavy, knobby end of his club. The blow sent the wolf flying sideways with a sharp yelp of pain. But hunger drove the wolf. As soon as it hit the ground, it gathered its feet and sprung forward for another attack.

Whack! Again the wolf went sprawling, dazed from a second sharp blow. Blood flowed from a gash in the side of its head. The shepherd was tempted to take advantage of the moment and spring on the wolf to finish it off, but it would be too dangerous to leave the open doorway to the sheep pen unguarded. So he stood his ground and waited.

The wolf pulled itself back to its feet, still growling, but it kept its distance, prowling along the edge of the campfire, staring at the shepherd and the sheep beyond, looking for some kind of opening. The shepherd stared back, club at the ready. The wolf glanced warily at the club, shook its head as if trying to clear the cobwebs out, whimpered, and then slipped back out into the darkness.

The shepherd continued to watch and listen, staying alert. But soon the sheep behind him began to settle down, a good sign that they no longer sensed danger. He let his tightened muscles begin to relax and then lay back down across the opening to the sheep pen. As long as he was there, serving as the door, the sheep were secure.

The next morning, the shepherd stood and stretched his body to work out the stiffness of the night. He then called each of his sheep by name. One by one they came out of the pen and followed him as he led them to green pastures. It was as if nothing had happened the night before, and as far as the sheep were concerned, nothing did. They were safe with the shepherd.

# FEAR FACTOR

## In the Word

Read John 10:1-21.

Fear and anxiety – they are robbers and thieves, stealing our peace, destroying our joy and spoiling our health. And these thieves seem to always be right outside the door, ready to barge in if we open it a crack. What would a week without fear and anxiety be like? How about a day? How about an hour? Some of us would be ecstatic for just ten minutes free from fear and anxiety. Oh, how we desire the feeling of being secure.

Security is what Jesus brings us. He is both the "good shepherd" and "the door" (shepherds sometimes acted as doors, sleeping across the opening of the sheep pen at night). Both images are pictures of security. We are secure because the Good Shepherd owns us, knows us by name, cares for us, and lays down His life for us. But it's not enough to know these things. In order to feel secure, we need to trust the Shepherd, and that can only be accomplished by spending time with the Shepherd.

## Julie Battenfield's Story

Dogs. Car accidents. Cancer. These are just a few of the things on Julie's long list of fears. "A lot of things scare me," she admits. "Constantly realizing that I have very little control over those things is hard."

And now with five teenagers in the house, topping her list is the fear she feels every time one of her kids leaves the house and gets behind the wheel to drive somewhere. "It's terrifying," says Julie. "It's like no other fear. I hear people joke about it, but I have never been so terrified. I wasn't even this scared of them dying of SIDS."

At those times when her fear threatens to derail her, Julie comes back to what she knows. "God is big. He's strong. He's good. He's all of those things you sing about and know in your head. But then you get to know them in your heart." Julie has complete confidence that when she sends her kids out into the world, no matter what happens to them, God is in control.

She often recognizes her fear first as a physical sensation, beginning with a rush of adrenaline that can make her feel a little sick to her stomach, give her a headache, make her feel jittery, or make her want to eat ice cream. Then she remembers the verse that says, "Do not be anxious for anything, but in everything, by prayer and petition, with thanksgiving, present your requests to God. And the peace of God, which transcends all understanding, will guard your hearts and your minds in Christ Jesus" (Philippians 4:6-7).

So once again Julie comes back to what she knows. "I know that He loves me and I know I love Him. Then I can feel His presence, and I become more clear-headed. The anxious voices stop. And when my mind is focused on God and His truth, then the physical and emotional sensations follow and I get calmer."

Becoming a mother has been one of the most significant tools God has used to teach Julie more about who He is and how much she can trust Him. Like many women, Julie had her dreams of what it would be like to be married and start a family. When she and Scott were married, it seemed her dreams would come true. But their first son, Josh, came sooner than they planned. So once they started the "baby train" as she calls it, they decided to keep going and have one or two more. After their third child was born, Julie thought they were done. She was content with two boys and a girl.

Then she found out she was pregnant again. This really wasn't in her plans, but she surrendered her plans to God and trusted He would give her the strength she needed to be a mother of four...until the day the doctor discovered two sets of heartbeats. Julie went from being the busy mom of three young children, to being the sleep-deprived mother of five children ages five and under. This was definitely not in her plans.

"At the time," says Julie, "it was terrifying and upsetting – so *not* in my plans, not even a little bit." Even more upsetting than having her plans completely rearranged, was the effect motherhood was having on Julie as a person. It was like God was "shining a spotlight on all of my character flaws. All the things I thought I had together—I really did *not* have together," says Julie. "It was painfully obvious."

One of those painful character flaws was Julie's desire to be in control and to have life go the way she wanted. "I had a selfish tendency," she admits. "It might not have always been apparent to others because I can put on a good face, but it's obvious to me, like when I start to feel resentful or discontentment seizes me."

Julie can see how God has used the circumstances of her life to reshape her character. He's helping her release her desire to be in control, surrender her fear of things that might happen, and trust God even when she doesn't understand Him.

Aside from daily using her role as a mother to teach these lessons, God used a painful time in Julie's life ten years ago. The twins had just turned three and a half and she was finally through the baby years. She could breathe again. She wasn't as sleep deprived. Everyone could get a glass of water for themselves and everyone was out of diapers.

That was when Julie's mom was diagnosed with cancer, and died just several months later. "I felt very entitled that this should not happen to me or my mom. And of course it shouldn't," Julie says. "It shouldn't happen to anyone." As Julie wrestled with God about this, she began to do what she calls "a character study on God." It took time, but on the other side of that Julie emerged with a much deeper relationship with Christ than ever before. "I've always believed that He loves me. That didn't change. But now there was a depth to it I hadn't realized before," she explains.

Julie came to see the parent-child relationship as a great picture of what it means to relate to God. When kids are toddlers, they are constantly asking "Why?" And no amount of explaining will necessarily make sense to a toddler. At some point, they've just got to trust that their parent loves them and knows best. Julie still has many questions for God, but she has peace that one day she will have answers.

She smiles when she thinks of her own mom with Christ in heaven. "My mom always talked about her 'why' list for God. And I just imagine ten years later that she's still asking questions, saying 'Okay, I'm almost done...'"

In the meantime, Julie is learning to trust God more each day. "It's not about getting my prayers answered the way I want – in fact, I'm still struggling to align my prayers to His. But I'm learning to be in His presence no matter what is happening." This is what gives Julie the confidence to walk by faith, not by sight.

## Make it Personal

- What do you learn about the character of Jesus, the Good Shepherd, in John 10:1-21? How does this give you confidence in facing the "wolves" in your life?

- John 10:10 says that the thief comes only to steal, kill and destroy. Fear and anxiety are certainly thieves, robbing us of the peace Christ offers. In what ways have you experienced fear or anxiety recently? What triggered those feelings?

- How do you normally respond when fear arises? What can you learn from Julie's story about how to battle fear in the future?

- John 10:4 says that the sheep follow the Good Shepherd because they know His voice. Recognizing the voice of the Shepherd comes from spending time with Him. In what ways have you heard the Shepherd speak to you recently? What is He calling you to?

- How has Jesus spoken to you in this devotional time?

## Prayer

Dear Jesus, thank you that I don't have to face the "wolves" in my life alone. I know you are my Good Shepherd and you are always with me. Please give me your peace today and help me to trust that you will lead me, protect me, and provide for me. Amen.

# UNCHAINED

## In the Word

Read John 10:7-10 and Psalm 103:1-12.

Our past can haunt us. The shame and guilt we feel over past sins can make us feel insecure and worthless today. Bad relationships from the past can poison current ones. We have all experienced how the past can damage and even destroy our present. That is what Satan, the thief, wants.

Satan will play the "remember when" game with us. He will hurl at us his accusations and lies. "Remember when you did that?" "And you call yourself a Christian?" "God is disgusted with you!" "Why do you think you can serve God after the kinds of things you've done?" "You're an embarrassment to God." Blow after blow, accusation after accusation, and lie by lie, Satan tries to keep us pinned down.

But Jesus is the gate and Satan is not allowed into Jesus' sheepfold. Jesus' sheep can "come in and go out, and find pasture" without a worry. That's the difference Jesus' presence can make, but only when we trust that "as far as the east is from the west, so far has he removed our transgressions from us."

## Vicki Newman

It's a day Vicki will never forget. "I was basically standing there naked. Naked and in chains," she says. That day all of her past mistakes came back to haunt her – and there were plenty of mistakes to be reminded of.

As a teenager, Vicki lived a wild life. A life filled with alcohol, drugs, parties, and boys. A life that caused her a great deal of shame and guilt.

Vicki knew she needed a Savior. "When I finally came to the end of myself," she remembers, "I said to God 'I need you to lead me and help me make good choices with my life.'" So at the age of nineteen, Vicki said yes to Jesus. As she began walking with Him, she learned what a godly relationship with a man was supposed to look like – so when she fell in love with Brent, a strong Christian and a man of integrity, she knew she wanted to spend her life with him.

Now, Vicki had it all, a growing relationship with the God who loved her, and a growing relationship with a husband who adored her. But there was trouble brewing. "I was still pretty self-absorbed," says Vicki. "Life was still all about me."

Not only that, but Vicki's past kept rearing its ugly head. She still carried the wounds inflicted on her by unfaithful boyfriends who treated her like an object. She felt chained to the past, and this was affecting her marriage. Every time she and Brent would have a conflict, she would blow it out of proportion. She found it impossible to trust him. In fact, deep down, she expected that at some point he would leave her – just as every past boyfriend had done.

During this time, Vicki was blessed to have an older Christian woman mentoring her in her faith. This woman amazed Vicki. "I looked at her life and saw the impact she had on other people's lives, the way she loved her husband and children, the words she said – and I wanted that," says Vicki. Even though her mentor was suffering with cancer, she was still able to care for others. "I knew she loved Jesus, so I knew that was the key. But I couldn't get there because I had this selfishness preventing me from going further."

Vicki's longing to have the kind of life and faith she saw in her mentor led her on a journey of going deeper with God. She read a book that caused her to examine how all the past hurts she had experienced were still holding onto her. So one tearful afternoon, Vicki made a list – a list of every sin, every failure, and every embarrassment. She detailed all the things she had been involved with before coming to Christ.

Her hope was that the list would help her finally be set free from the past. But after filling four pages with her shame and guilt, Vicki was so devastated that she shoved the list in her Bible and said, "I'm not going any further with this." Time went by and Vicki forgot about the list – until that day she stood naked in chains, following a memorial service at her church.

After a painful battle with cancer, Vicki's mentor had died. Vicki's heart was broken by the loss of her friend. But her heart almost stopped beating altogether when the pastor came up to her after the service and mentioned finding THE list. Vicki was horrified. Apparently the list had fallen out of her Bible and her pastor found it. She was so deeply ashamed that this godly man had read about every single one of her sins. She didn't know how to respond. "He knew everything," she remembers. "And there I stood, basically naked in front of him."

That's when her pastor spoke the words of truth that changed Vicki's life forever. "You've done business with God," he said. "Now this list is as far from you as the east is from the west. These things hold no power over you any longer."

"The chains fell off right there," says Vicki. "I walked away a free woman – free from the guilt and shame of the choices and actions and filth that I had done." From that point forward, Vicki began to live into the truth of who she was in Christ – a new creation, no longer held by the past.

Her husband noticed an almost immediate change in her. Whenever conflict would arise, they could talk about the real issues rather than needing to go all the way back and deal with Vicki's trust issues and wounds from the past. Vicki also found herself freed up to take her eyes off of herself and think more about others. "My life from that point forward was about not just my needs," she says, "but about others."

It's been more than twenty years since the chains fell off, and God has continued to help Vicki live in the truth of her freedom. "It's been a shedding of untruth, of lies that I accumulated," she says. "As I spend time with Him, reading His Word, listening to Him, His Spirit comes in to reveal things and meet my needs. There's been incredible healing and freedom in that." The life Vicki always wanted, the life she saw in her mentor all those years ago, is now hers as she surrenders more of herself to Christ.

## Make it Personal

- Have you ever had an experience like Vicki – of being "found out," having someone else discover a shameful secret about you? How did that feel? If you've never experienced this, put yourself in Vicki's shoes for a moment and imagine what that would be like. What would it be like to have someone speak such words of grace to you, as her pastor did?

- Psalm 103:10-12 shows us that God does not treat us as our sins deserve. How do you think you deserve to be treated by God? What does this passage reveal about how God actually treats us?

- In John 10:10, Jesus says that He has come to give us life – to the full. When you picture life to the full, what comes to mind? How can any sin – no matter how big or small – hinder that life?

- How has Jesus spoken to you in this devotional time?

## Prayer

Dear Jesus, please help me to come clean with you today and receive your forgiveness. Help me not to keep living in past guilt and shame, but to find freedom through you today. Please remove any chains that are holding me back from living life to the full in you. Amen.

# A STRONG GRIP

## In the Word

Read John 10:24-30 and Romans 8:35-39.

Jesus knows you by name. He knows every problem you face. And He knows what's ahead. Jesus also knows every member of your family and every issue they are facing. Jesus knows it all. He knows every little thing you could possibly worry about and He can see the bigger picture that you cannot see.

Not only does Jesus know you, but he has a solid grip on you. Do you feel like you are going under? Jesus has a grip on you. Do you feel lost? Jesus has a grip on you. Are you facing a temptation? Jesus has a grip on you. Are you grieving? Jesus has a grip on you. And nothing can break that grip! Remember that, claim that, embrace that the next time you start to worry.

## Laura Volinsky's Story

Does anyone know what "normal" is? According to Laura, "normal is just a setting on your dryer." She laughs when she says this, because as the mother of four teenagers – three with special needs – she had to let go of her notions of "normal" a long time ago.

She remembers having a conversation with God many years ago to discuss her feelings of being overloaded with problems. She yelled at God, telling Him that this wasn't her dream for her life and family. "I kept asking Him, 'Why me?'" she says. But over time, her prayer changed from "Why me, God? This is too hard!" to "Why me, God? Why did you choose me to get to take care of these angels?"

Laura admits that she has struggled with worry and wanting to have control. "We worry because we fear losing control," she explains. In those moments when worry threatens to take over, Laura reminds herself of her favorite verse from Philippians 4:13, which says, "I can do all things through Christ who strengthens me." This helps her remember that she can only do all things *through Christ.*

She also remembers that Christ has answered her prayers so many times in the past – *whether she worried or not.* In other words, her worry accomplished nothing more than making her sick to her stomach. And God was still in control either way.

"People say I smile all the time and that I carry the kids' disabilities well," says Laura. "But that's not always true. I'm not a super Christian." Laura is still learning how to surrender control to Christ, recognizing that "God has never failed me – so why worry now?"

These days Laura finds her thoughts drifting to the future, wondering what is going to happen to her boys as they get older. "There are so many things I'm not sure about, things that I need to put into place for our sons. There's so much about the future that I could worry about. One of our sons is going to need a lot more help to finish high school, and then what will come next for him? And our son Caleb is not always going to live with us, so who will provide for him?" she wonders.

Three of her four boys are on the autism spectrum, but Caleb, her sixteen-year-old, is the most severe. He needs help with everything. He cannot speak, he still wears pull-ups, and he can only walk short distances. While Laura has some in-home caregivers to help, she knows there will come a time when they will need to find a more long-term place for Caleb to live.

But every time Laura is tempted to start worrying about what the future holds, she remembers how God has been there in the past. In the past, every time they needed a new caregiver, Laura says, "I would freak out. But every time God provided just the right person at just the right time."

She knows that God wants her to be responsible and make plans for the future. "But when I find myself going too far into the future and worrying, I put the brakes on and remember – God, you have not failed me yet," says Laura. "He is helping me to live in the present and not worry about the future."

In the process of overcoming worry, Laura has learned more about how big God is. For years she prayed that Caleb would at least be able to talk. "My thought was that a child isn't really a child unless they could talk," Laura remembers. "Then God changed my heart and helped me get Caleb out of the box I had him in. God said to me, 'This is Caleb – this is who he is. Whoever you're talking about, whoever you want Caleb to be, that's not who I made him to be.'"

As Laura's heart toward Caleb began to change, God gave her new eyes with which to see him. "Now, when I see Caleb, he just makes me smile. And I've seen that God is different than what I thought – He's much bigger." Laura surrendered her desire to change Caleb, and in the process she herself was changed.

Laura sees how Caleb is dependent on her for everything. He is surrendered to her, whether he wants to be or not. And this reminds her that she can't be the parent she needs to be unless she's surrendered to her heavenly Father. "The worship song, 'I'm Running to Your Arms' means so much to me right now," says Laura. "I picture myself running into the arms of God, like our kids do with us."

Her growing relationship with God is helping Laura let go of her striving and her worry. And best of all, says Laura, "There's hope for the future, but also peace for the present."

## Make it Personal

- Like Laura, what images of a "normal" life have you had to surrender? How has this experience changed you? Changed your relationship with God?

- In John 10:24-30, Jesus reminds us that He knows us, and that no one can snatch us out of His hand. In what ways does this knowledge give you comfort or confidence today?

- Consider what types of circumstances in your life threaten to pull you away from God's love at times. Read Romans 8:35-39 and reflect on how the truth of these verses can help when you feel yourself being pulled away from God.

- How has Jesus spoken to you in this devotional time?

## Prayer

Dear Jesus, thank you for the assurance that you will never leave me or forsake me. Thank you for your promise to walk with me through all the ups and downs of my life. Hold me close today and fill me with your love. Amen.

# PRIDE in OWNERSHIP

## In the Word

Read John 10:11-18.

Jesus makes it clear – He is not the hired hand. The hired hand is not invested in the sheep. The hired hand will not risk his life for something that does not belong to him. The hired hand does not care for the sheep the way the owner does.

Jesus is not the hired hand, He's our owner. Jesus takes personal responsibility for each of us. He loves each of us, cares for each of us, enjoys each of us, is proud of each of us, guides each of us, feeds each of us, and lays down his life for each of us. There are no outcasts in Jesus' sheepfold.

When you put your life in the Shepherd's hands you are owned, and that makes all the difference.

## Susan's Story

Susan's smile is contagious and she has a friendly and talkative personality to match. She seems like a typical high school senior – but her life has been anything but typical. In fact, it's a miracle she's even alive.

Susan's birth parents were both drug addicts. By the time she was born, her father was nowhere to be found and her mother was in no condition to care for a baby, so Susan was put up for adoption. She was soon placed with a couple, but it wasn't a loving home.

"I remember my mom trying to drown me in a bathtub and hitting me with a shoe," Susan shares. Her parents also kept her in a closet and only fed her one meal a day. Susan was eight years old before Child Protective Services caught wind of what was happening to her. When they removed her from the home, she was severely malnourished, weighing only 20% of what a child her height should weigh.

Susan spent the next four years in a foster home. Those were equally difficult years for her. Because of her previous mistreatment, she was socially awkward and extremely shy. "The kids at school saw me as an easy target," Susan remembers. "So they teased, ridiculed and bullied me."

Rejected by her birth parents, abused and neglected by her foster parents and now bullied by her classmates, Susan felt utterly rejected, unwanted, unloved and worthless. She saw no purpose or reason for her life and she started to have frequent thoughts about suicide, but fortunately she never acted on them.

Susan's social worker realized that a change was needed, so she placed Susan into a foster-to-adopt program where, if everything went well, the foster parent would become the adoptive parent. After filling out a profile, Susan was matched with a prospective parent, a single woman named Mary.

The two of them hit it off remarkably fast. They both agree that it only took a matter of months to build a mother-daughter relationship of love and trust. Maybe it was because Susan was so hungry for love and affirmation, and Mary gave her plenty. "For the first time in my life, I felt wanted and loved," Susan shares. The icing on the cake was that she was starting at a different school. The bullies were left behind.

Mary began taking Susan to church. It was the first time in her life that she had gone to church. When Susan showed up for the middle school youth group, she was warmly welcomed by the leaders. "I kept coming back every week because each week I would get a big hug from my small group leader," Susan says, smiling as she describes the high school gal who volunteered to work with the middle school girls.

Each week Susan would hear about the love of Jesus and the message resonated with her. She remembers one night singing a song that talked about not being worthless or alone because Jesus is with you. Then in their Bible study, Psalm 139:13-14 was shared. "For you created my inmost being; you knit me together in my mother's womb. I praise you because I am fearfully and wonderfully made; your works are wonderful, I know that full well."

"I realized that I wasn't a reject," Susan shares. She began to see that in God's eyes she was made perfect. She decided to give her life to Jesus Christ and become His follower.

"Jesus has changed me so much," Susan shares. And Mary, now her adopted mom, wholeheartedly agrees. "I used to steal, lie and gossip like no other," Susan remembers. "I was one of those mean girls, because that's what I thought people wanted. It was what I saw on T.V." Now the stealing and lying have stopped. So has the gossiping, although she admits it took a long time to break that habit.

Susan is also no longer a wallflower. It turns out that Susan is naturally extroverted, but the neglect she suffered had made her painfully shy and introverted. As she experienced love and acceptance, her sense of worth began to blossom, and her confidence grew. "I used to never talk to anyone, but now I am the one to go up and introduce myself to newcomers," she says. It's a remarkable transformation.

"I've also discovered my purpose," Susan shares enthusiastically. Maybe she is most excited about this because she still remembers those painful years when she contemplated suicide, feeling that her life had no purpose. "I discovered that I love being around kids," she says. Susan has become a highly valued volunteer at her church, where she works with young kids.

What's most special about Susan's love for kids is what she wants to do with this gift. "I want to become a social worker," she says. "Because of what I've gone through, I can tell kids, 'I've been through what you're going through. You're not alone.' I can make a difference in their lives. I feel like this is my calling."

"At first, I was mad at God because of all I've gone through," Susan says. "But then I realized how much God has blessed me with a new mom, new friends, and a new life." Susan realizes how much Jesus has changed her, and how He has redeemed a terrible past and turned it into something that gives her strength and purpose – a way to be a blessing to others.

To meet this bubbly, talkative, and confident teenager you would never guess that she is the product of rejection. But love has changed Susan. Because of the love of Jesus, her mom, and her church, Susan is growing into the beautiful young woman God created her to be.

## Make it Personal

- As you read John 10:11-18, how does it make you feel to know that Jesus, the Good Shepherd, is willing to fight for you and lay down His life for you?

- When have you seen an example of the difference between someone with ownership and someone who is merely a hired hand? (Perhaps you've seen this in your workplace or even your church.)

- Susan experienced abandonment and rejection by people in her life who were merely hired hands. But when she finally found a loving home, church, and relationship with Jesus, she began to experience God's love and ownership. Where in your life have you had a negative experience with a hired hand versus someone who really loved you and invested in you? How does this give you a window into what Jesus is teaching about in today's passage?

- How has Jesus spoken to you in this devotional time?

## Prayer

Dear Jesus, you are truly the Good Shepherd. It's hard for me to grasp the love you have for me, a love that would literally lay down your life for me. Thank you for being a true owner, not merely a hired hand. Help me to honor your ownership of my life today by following you closely. Amen.

# Day 26

# ETERNAL PERSPECTIVE

## In the Word

Read Psalm 23, Psalm 27:1, and John 10:28.

When you are aware of the presence of the Good Shepherd, there is a tremendous sense of comfort and peace. You are able to relax and to rest, to be confident and courageous, to enjoy and to bless. When you are weak, you are aware of His strength. When you are hurting, you are aware of His comfort. When you are lonely, you are aware of His love.

When you are aware of His presence, you are also certain about your future, and that, too, offers tremendous comfort and security. When we can see things from the perspective of eternity, our troubles become momentary and our losses become temporary. And to those who are securely in the grip of Christ, death doesn't carry the same fearsome threat.

When the Lord is your Shepherd, you truly shall not be in want of hope, security, strength, comfort, joy, peace, confidence, love, and so much more.

## Donna Chapman's Story

Donna will never forget that day. When she heard the news about Tammy, her daughter, it changed her life forever.

Earlier that morning, Tammy had stopped to get gas on the way to church – it was the last thing she would ever do on this earth. When Tammy got out of her car, a stranger, a paranoid schizophrenic who had stopped taking his medication, walked up and stabbed her in the chest, killing her instantly. He then reached into her purse, took out $20 and walked up to pay for his gas. He later told police that he didn't have any money, so (to his clouded mind) the obvious thing to do was to take it from someone else. Tammy just happened to be at the wrong place at the wrong time.

Where do you turn when something so sudden, so shocking and so wrong happens?

Donna had grown up as a Jehovah's Witness, but as a young adult decided she didn't believe their teachings. Since her mom was a devout Jehovah's Witness, Donna felt it would create too much tension if she started going to church elsewhere, so she stopped going altogether. However, her daughter Tammy started to go to church with a friend. At the age of sixteen, Tammy put her faith in Jesus and became a faithful follower from then on.

Donna was happy for her daughter, but Christianity wasn't for her. Going to church took too much time. She had more important things to do, like work – which is where she was that Sunday morning when her precious daughter, who was a wife and mother, was murdered.

When Donna's husband gave her the news, "I went into shock," she remembers. "At first it didn't compute. As we drove to Tammy's home to be with her husband and our grandchildren, I was still trying to comprehend what had happened. Our daughter was healthy and vibrant, a good person, a good wife and mom, and she was on her way to church. I just couldn't believe it was true."

It wasn't until Donna went inside Tammy's home, where other relatives had started gathering, that the reality hit home and the tears started to flow.

Later that afternoon, she retreated to Tammy's bedroom to be alone for awhile. She had finished calling close friends and relatives, having to repeat over and over again the words, "Tammy is dead," each call reinforcing the horrible truth. Now she was alone with her thoughts. "At that moment, I felt something like a warm blanket being wrapped around me," she says.

Donna knows now that this warmth, which she could tangibly feel, were the hundreds, maybe thousands of prayers being prayed for her at that very moment. The word was quickly spreading through Tammy's church. Friends were calling friends, prayer chains were being alerted, emails were being sent, and people were praying.

And those prayers made a real difference in Donna's life. She didn't react to the whole event the way many might have expected. Even though her precious daughter had been murdered in a random act of violence, Donna didn't become angry at God.

"I had always known that Tammy had a living relationship with Jesus," Donna explains. "I knew Jesus was real because I could see it in my daughter – I just never had time for Jesus myself. But when Tammy was killed, I had no doubt that Tammy was in heaven with Jesus, and that comforted me."

The next Sunday, Donna attended the worship service at Tammy's church. God spoke to her through the message that was shared, and at the end of the message she prayed and asked Jesus to become her Savior. It was a watershed moment.

From that moment on, Donna poured herself into falling in love with Jesus. She had always been an avid reader, but she never had time to read the Bible – there were too many other novels to read. Now she didn't have time to read anything but the Bible. She joined multiple Bible study groups and took Grief Care classes at the church. There was so much about God to discover, she was like a sponge soaking it all in. And she was amazed by how much love she received from people.

Tammy had been registered to go to a church women's retreat with her Bible study group. Now Tammy's group invited Donna to come in Tammy's place. It was a special time of healing for everyone.

Often a parent will pass their faith on to their children. But for Donna it worked the other way around. Tammy's legacy now lives on through her mother. Tammy's faith gave Donna just enough faith to keep from getting angry at God. Then, after experiencing that supernatural feeling of comfort in Tammy's bedroom, Donna found Jesus for herself and was changed.

It's been six years since Donna lost her daughter, and she continues to grow in her faith and to allow Christ to shape her character. "Before following Christ, I used to think mostly of myself," says Donna. "And I didn't have much time or compassion for strangers or people who were less fortunate than me. In fact, I always thought of homeless people as bums who were too lazy to get a job."

Donna is clearly a new creation in Christ. God has softened her heart and she is more caring than ever. If Donna sees a homeless person, she now takes the time to stop and help him – to the amazement of some of her old friends. She has also become an effervescent dynamo, always ready to serve someone in need, to offer a word of encouragement, and to support those who are suffering from a loss. Far from being angry and bitter, Donna is filled with love and energy.

When asked what she would say if she could tell her daughter one thing, Donna says, " I would tell her, 'Look Tammy, I'm going to church!'" Donna laughs when she imagines how Tammy would respond. "She would be doing the Funky Chicken!"

## Make it Personal

- Psalm 23 is a famous Psalm describing what life is like when the Lord is your Shepherd. What elements of this Psalm invite you today? In what ways today might the Lord want you to allow Him to be more fully your Good Shepherd?

- Read John 10:28. If you are a Christian, what confidence does this verse provide for your life here on earth?

- In today's story, we read how Tammy left a legacy by living out her faith in Christ, making it easy for her mother to know that Jesus is real. If you were to die today, what kind of legacy would you leave? Who has God called you to pray for and share His love with so that they, too, can know that Jesus is real?

- How has Jesus spoken to you in this devotional time?

## Prayer

Dear Jesus, thank you that I can have confidence of spending eternity with you. Help me to remember that this earth is not my home, and to live each day to the full in you. Use me to share your love with those around me so that they can know that you are real and follow you, too. Amen.

# HEARING the VOICE

## In the Word

Read John 10:3-5, 27.

We have the unique ability of recognizing the voices of the people we love. We hear our child's voice stand out in a noisy playground or a friend's laugh from a distance. We can pick these voices out because we have spent a good deal of time with these people and paid special attention to them.

Jesus said that His sheep will listen and follow His voice. In fact, that is the defining characteristic of His sheep. And as you have learned this week, listening to and following the Shepherd leads to blessings.

We learn to recognize God's voice by spending time with Him and paying special attention. It starts with the Bible, but it's not enough to just read it. We need to follow what it says. The more we obey, the more Jesus' voice will stand out. And the more we obey, the more we will enjoy the green pastures of life that the Shepherd is guiding us towards.

## Brent & Vicki Newman's Story

Christ is alive and well in the Newman's marriage – and it's a good thing, too. Brent shares that "after 24 years, our marriage could have ended a long, long time ago if not for Christ."

People who know them well might think that's an overstatement, since their marriage seems so solid. But Brent and Vicki are confident that the presence of Jesus Christ has made all the difference. Brent has been with the California Highway Patrol for nearly 25 years, and when he sees guys at work who are on their second or third wife, it reminds him how important it is to follow God's ways for marriage. "I'm glad to say that I'm still on my first wife," he smiles, "and I hope to stay that way."

Vicki smiles, too, as she remembers the early days of their married life when Brent was gone for six months at the CHP's live-in academy. "There were all these emotional needs that I expected Brent to meet," she shares, "and all of a sudden he was gone. I remember so many nights being alone, missing him and feeling insecure."

Vicki began listening to sermons on the radio in the evenings, and she came to understand how much she really needed God to fill her needs. This truth became especially apparent to her when they moved to Los Angeles for Brent's first assignment. "Not knowing when he would be home and knowing that he was out on the streets of LA – I was lonely and scared," she says. "But Jesus was right there with me, and He met those needs my husband couldn't meet."

As she continues to seek Christ first in her life, it has also strengthened her marriage. "Throughout the seasons of life – the moves, the career changes, the kids, the different emotional issues we've had to deal with – I've continued going to Christ with my needs," says Vicki. "I love my husband, I really do!" ("Whew!" says Brent.) Vicki laughs and goes on to say that "although I love him, I can't expect him to meet all my needs. My relationship with Christ is a well from which I can draw to satisfy that thirst within me for love, security, healing, and strength in dealing with the day-to-day stuff."

"There's a paradox here," says Brent, "because the closer she walks with the Lord, the less needy she becomes, and the more I'm capable of meeting her needs." Brent is quick to say that he needs to be seeking Christ as well. "After all, men have needs, too." ("Now we've got that on tape!" Vicki teases.) "It's true," Brent says, giving Vicki a playful squeeze. "It only took me twenty years to admit it."

Watching them together, it's easy to see how Christ is working both in their individual lives and in their marriage. Vicki observes that "As we grow in our relationship with Christ, we see more fruit of the Spirit – things like kindness, joy, goodness, peace, faithfulness, and love – things that really enrich a marriage."

"That's right," Brent continues, "when you're walking with the Lord, you can't help but grow toward Him. He literally reshapes your thoughts and turns the things that are upside-down in your life, right-side up." But when Brent talks about walking with the Lord, he makes it clear that he's not talking about something nebulous. It involves some very specific actions on his part, including a daily time of reading scripture, praying, and seeking God's wisdom.

"Ultimately, it's not just learning about Jesus as if you're learning about a topic," Brent explains. "It's about having a relationship with someone who is really real, even though he's not physically present. This centers me, draws me back to the right principles, and keeps my priorities straight on a daily basis."

Brent is clear about how this affects his marriage. "As I walk with Christ, it makes a huge difference in how I am with Vicki. It's the difference between me superficially listening when she's sharing something and thinking 'get to the point and let me solve your problem,' versus Christ helping me to *actually* listen. This is not a natural skill for a lot of us guys. I can listen beyond just the surface content. I can listen for her meaning, really caring about what she says. That doesn't just happen naturally without Christ's help."

"Not that our marriage is all puppy dogs and butterflies," he goes on. "It's not like there's never any conflict. Sometimes there are serious things we need to talk about." But Brent and Vicki agree that going to God first makes all the difference.

One way Vicki has learned to do this is by modeling her prayers after many of the Psalms. "Since the time I was young, I've loved the Psalms because they're authentic, interactive prayers. The attitudes of the writers are those of submission and honesty. So sometimes when I get angry with Brent, I write my own Psalm to God," she explains. "When I'm stuck, I might write something like 'I'm so mad at him!'"

Brent enjoys Vicki's prayer practice and says, "She tells me that she's been tattling on me to the Lord. And after she's done this, I can see a transformation in her heart. It's not like you're just praying to the air – it's a real relationship, and you can see the transformation taking place."

When Brent and Vicki were first married, like many couples they expected that they would find fulfillment through their spouse. Over the years, they have learned that their true fulfillment comes through their individual and mutual relationships with Jesus Christ. That's the glue that holds them together. And others are taking notice. God has begun using Brent and Vicki to counsel with couples needing help in their marriage.

"If you aren't choosing to walk with Christ and love your spouse," says Brent, "then you should expect that things aren't going to go well. Thankfully, it's easy to fix. Return to God, and return to choosing to love your spouse."

## Make it Personal

- Brent and Vicki share some of the ways they are intentional about building their individual relationships with Christ. What kinds of intentional practices are helpful to you in building your relationship with Him? Are there any practices that Brent and Vicki mention that you might like to try? Which ones?

- In today's passage, we read that when we are a follower of Jesus, we will learn to recognize His voice so that we can follow Him. What are some ways that you recognize His voice these days? What helps you discern if it's His voice or the voice of someone else?

- We can't recognize Jesus' voice if we're not even taking time to listen. How might you spend some time today listening for the voice of Jesus?

- How has Jesus spoken to you in this devotional time?

## Prayer

Dear Jesus, I know that you gave me one mouth and two ears for a reason – please help me to spend more time listening to you and less time talking. Teach me how to follow you and walk in your ways. Amen.

# Day 28

## a spiritual practice
# LECTIO DIVINA Praying the Word

Lectio Divina ("Holy Reading" in Latin) is a centuries-old practice of meditating on, and praying through a scripture passage. Any brief passage of scripture can be used for this practice. However, in keeping with this week's theme of Jesus as the Good Shepherd, we recommend that you use Psalm 23.

## Silencio – Remember

Begin with a time of preparation. Sit comfortably. Relax your body. Acknowledge and release distractions. Invite God's presence. Take a few deep breaths, and with each in-breath become aware of God's love for you. With each out-breath let go of whatever might distract you from listening.

## Lectio – Read

Slowly and meditatively read the verses through as a whole. What word or phrase beckons you, stirs you, unnerves you? You don't need to think about what it means just yet. Simply pay attention to any word or phrase that attracts your attention. Don't analyze or judge at this point. Just be open to the words and to the One who speaks through the Word. After reading, pause for a moment and sit silently with the word or phrase that drew your attention. (*Note: If you are doing Lectio with a small group or with your family, allow for 1-2 minutes of silence after the reading. Then invite people to share, without comment, the word or phrase that attracted them.*)

## Meditatio – Reflect

Read the passage again. This time, listen for God's invitation to you. How does this reading touch your life today? Do not try to force a meaning. Stay open. This is a time of reflection involving thinking, feeling, and/or intuition. Be aware of inner resistance. Open your heart and will to the action that you may be called to. After the reading, pause again to reflect on how the reading speaks into your life today. (*Note: If you are doing this with a group, you may want to have a different person read this time.*)

## Oratio – Respond

Read one more time. Continue to chew on the word and let its flavor penetrate your heart. How does God want you to respond? After the reading, spend a few moments telling God how you feel about what you have heard, understood or felt. Be as honest as you are able; don't try to protect God (as if that were even possible). Listen for a response. And then continue in the dialogue with God. Pray yourself empty. (*If you're doing this with a group, you may want to have a different person read.*)

## Contemplatio – Resting

Simply be with God, letting God make a home in you. Drop into God's presence beneath all your thoughts and feelings. Rest completely in God, grateful for what has been given and what you were able to receive. (*Note: If you are doing this with a group, take time after the last step to share aloud the word, image or invitation you received. Pray for God to help the person next to you to respond to the invitation and/or word received.*)

### Bible Passages for Lectio Divina
God can speak to us through any passage of scripture. However, for Lectio Divina, the Psalms can be an excellent place to begin. Choose a Psalm or portion of a Psalm and use it for your prayer time. Try to avoid overly-familiar passages to begin with so that you're less tempted to jump ahead in your mind. Also, it's best to choose a relatively short passage.

A few other great passages you may want to use in the beginning of this type of scripture prayer are: Psalm 63:1-7; John 3:1-10; Romans 12:1-2; Ephesians 1:15-22; Matthew 11:28-30; Colossians 1:15-20; Isaiah 55:1-2; Matthew 14:22-32; John 14:1-7; and James 1:2-8.

If you choose a familiar passage, try using a different translation than you would normally use, like the *New Living Translation* or *The Message*.

# Week 5

# "I Am the Resurrection and the Life"

Wiping a damp cloth across her brother's forehead, she thought, "The fever must be high." He was hot to the touch and his clothes were drenched with sweat, clinging to his skin. She looked at his drawn face, drained of color. He had lost so much weight so fast. For what must have been the thousandth time, her thoughts turned toward the Master, as she asked herself, "Where is He? Will He make it in time?"

She pictured her brother just a week ago, sitting at the dinner table, spraying wine as he unexpectedly laughed at one of her rare jokes. She wasn't much of a joke teller, so this one took him off guard. Then he looked at the mess he had made, and the spatters of red wine dotting his sister's shocked face, and started laughing even harder. They were all laughing until their stomachs ached from the strain.

She remembered the mirth dancing in Lazarus' deep brown eyes. How many times had she seen that familiar twinkle? That was one of the little things she loved that about her brother. But now the light was gone from his eyes. She sighed as she tried to get Lazarus to sip some water. "I hope He'll hurry."

Martha watched the life drain from her brother. The doctors had been in to see him and did what little they could. The Rabbi from the synagogue had stopped by to offer prayers. Yet her brother continued to decline. It had been going on for days. She had seen this before in others, and it seldom ended well. "I wonder how far away He is?"

As she lay in her bed listening to her brother's soft moans nearby, she thought of the life her brother should still have in front of him. "Will I ever see him get married? Will I ever get to hear the laughter of nieces and nephews? Will I ever see him grow old and become a respected elder, passing his wisdom on to younger generations?" Then she wondered again, "Did He get the message about Lazarus? Is He on His way?"

In the morning, her brother was worse, periodically going into shakes and then suddenly becoming very still. Then he gave a sudden, sharp cry, gasped, and was gone. Martha yelled, "No, Lazarus, wake up! No! Hang on! He's not here yet." Mary began to wail. Martha looked up in shock at her sister and then again at Lazarus. The moment seemed frozen in time. As reality swept over her, she slumped and buried her head in Lazarus' chest and began to sob.

It was another four days, before He showed up. The funeral was over. The body had been buried.

Martha went out to meet Him. She put on her brave face, but the accusation tumbled out before she could stop herself. "If only you had been here, my brother would not have died."

"Your brother will rise again," He assured her.

"I know he will rise again in the resurrection at the last day," she responded.

"Martha," Jesus said, "I *am* the resurrection and the life." He paused, staring into her eyes, bloodshot from crying, and then gently asked, "Do you believe this?"

# I NEED a MIRACLE

## In the Word

Read John 11:1-44.

The sisters were devastated by the death of their brother. They believed that Jesus could have done something if He had arrived sooner. But what could Jesus do in this present situation? It was too late. Lazarus was dead.

What Jesus did was to comfort with the words, "Your brother will rise again."

"Yes, I know that," Martha replied, "He will rise *in the future.*" It was a small comfort.

"Martha, I *am* the resurrection and the life! ...Do you believe this?" A few minutes later everyone learned what he meant.

Jesus' declaration continues to be a challenge and encouragement to us. When the Resurrection and the Life is present in our life, it's never too late. Resurrections, big and small, can happen at any time. Do you believe this?

## Joanna Quintrell's Story

Osteonecrosis. That was the big, scary word staring at Joanna from her email. That was the term that described the results of her MRI, and the explanation for the intense pain she was experiencing in her knee. And as a result of that condition, almost overnight Joanna became crippled.

Joanna learned that the word Osteonecrosis literally means, "bone death." For reasons the doctors couldn't explain, the blood supply to Joanna's knee was cut off, causing part of the bone around her knee to simply die. But strangely, she had none of the risk factors for this rare bone disease, such as alcoholism, steroid use, or AIDS.

Joanna was put on crutches and told not to put any weight on her leg. She couldn't even set her foot on the floor, because with dead bone in her knee, any pressure on the knee could cause the whole knee to crumble.

Suddenly, she felt like Dorothy in the Wizard of Oz. "One minute I'm in Kansas, just having my normal life," Joanna says, "and the next minute this tornado comes out of nowhere and BAM! I wake up in a different life."

Joanna is an active hiker and gardener, and she was no longer able to enjoy these life-giving activities. In fact, her doctor actually said, "You'll never hike again." That was a real blow for Joanna, who loves hiking such strenuous trails as Half Dome in Yosemite.

Now, not only did she have to learn how to accept her new reality, and learn how to navigate her world on crutches, but she also had to deal with enormous pain. "They say the pain of Osteonecrosis is second only to bone cancer," Joanna shares.

The doctor told Joanna that a likely result of this disease was that she would be crippled for the rest of her life. He also explained there was a very remote possibility that she might be healed. "Technically, it's possible that your body could heal itself," he explained. "It's possible that your body could send out new blood vessels, that it could lay down new bone, and that the new bone could be strengthened enough so that your knee will be fine, a process called 'revascularization'." However, the doctor said that the chances of "revascularization" were so minute that she should dismiss the thought. It was not going to happen.

But Joanna knew God has the power to heal her if He chose to. In fact, she runs a ministry in Santa Rosa called Journey Center, and one of the central elements of their ministry is healing prayer. So Joanna asked everyone she could think of to pray, and "revascularization" became the word that hundreds of people prayed for her knee.

As the weeks and months went by, Joanna did all she could to care for the health of her knee while staying close to God. But she also battled times of discouragement. "It was devastating," she shares. "And yet somehow you hang on to God's promises. And you think, 'I don't know what you're doing, God, or why this is happening, but I have to trust you.'"

Even in the midst of her turmoil and struggle, "there was this knowing that God was in control," Joanna says. "I was confident that He knows what He's doing, and if I'm supposed to be healed, I'll be healed." She learned to stay present to God, even in the midst of her pain. And although she prayed for healing, she didn't demand it.

During this time, Joanna was also unable to go into work at the Journey Center. "By eleven in the morning, I would be utterly and completely exhausted and have no energy for the rest of the day," she explains. Her exhaustion was partly a result of her lack of sleep, resulting from often waking up in the middle of the night with horrible cramps running from her hip all the way down to her foot.

After a year of living with Osteonecrosis, Joanna went in for another MRI to determine the status of her knee. When her chiropractor called with the results, he asked, "Are you sitting down?" She and her husband quickly sat down, and it's a good thing they did. "I just got your results," he said, "and it's gone!"

"What?" Joanna asked in disbelief. He went on to explain that the Osteonecrosis was completely gone. "We just sat there, stunned," she remembers. "We didn't even know what to say. I mean it's hardly real."

Joanna's chiropractor told her that the passage God had given him as he prayed faithfully for Joanna's knee, was the story from Ezekiel of the dry bones coming back to life. Throughout her illness, God also frequently reminded Joanna of a verse from Isaiah that says the lame will leap for joy.

The resurrection of Joanna's dead bone has certainly caused her heart to leap for joy. She would be the first to say she doesn't understand why God chose her for healing. She just sensed him say, "I'm not going to explain it to you. But I am going to tell you that I want to do this for you." Joanna says "That was almost like a different kind of healing – to have that personal touch from God."

As she thinks back on the past two years, Joanna says, "God encouraged me all the way along. Even if I hadn't been healed, I would tell you that God encouraged me. He met me in the midst of my upside-down life. He comforted me. He surrounded us with people and took care of us –

even when it was awful."

Joanna received the news of her healing in March of 2011, and it's been a long road since then. "I had lost so much muscle from not putting any weight on it. My one leg was about half the size of my other leg." So she has worked faithfully to rebuild her muscles, but it has been a joy to do so.

Joanna has also experienced the joy of returning to gardening and hiking. This past summer she and her husband took a three week trip up the West Coast, hiking three to seven miles a day. And her knee never hurt.

## Make it Personal

- Notice how Mary and Martha react to Jesus. What do they know about who Jesus is and what He can do? Why is this knowledge still not enough to prepare them for what He is about to do?

- To help us trust Jesus in the present, it can be helpful to remember what we know of Him from the past. How have you seen Him work in your life or the lives of others? How can knowing what Jesus can do, and has done, help you trust Him today?

- In today's story, how did Joanna deal with the devastating news that her world was being turned upside down? How did Mary and Martha each respond differently to the reality of their brother's death? How do you react when your world is turned upside-down?

- Look back at John 11:1-44 and focus on what Jesus says and does. What do you learn about His character? What insights does this give you regarding how He may be working in your life right now?

- How has Jesus spoken to you in this devotional time?

## Prayer

Dear Jesus, today I choose to trust you, even when I don't see what you're doing in my life. Strengthen my faith. Help me see that you are not just the God of the past or future, you are the God of right here and now. Amen.

# CONFUSED

## In the Word

Read John 11:1-6, 17-21.

Jesus dragged His feet. According to the Gospel of John, Jesus loved Lazarus very much, but He intentionally waited for him to die.

On the surface, this intentional delay is disturbing. Yes, we can see the bigger picture. Yes, we can see the reason for the delay. And yes, we know how the story ends. But put yourself in Mary and Martha's shoes – they couldn't have known what was going to happen. They were faced with a choice of whether or not they would still trust Jesus.

In our own lives there will be times when we will have to make the same choice. Things will happen that we do not understand. Things will be taken away from us. And through it all, God will seem to be missing.

These times will test our faith. Will we believe in Jesus even when things are not going our way? Will we believe that He sees the bigger picture? Will we trust that we will experience His resurrection and life, even though everything at the moment seems to be dying?

## Daphne DeMaris' Story

Daphne was living comfortably. She had a successful practice as a Marriage and Family Therapist and a nice place to live in an upper middle class suburb of Detroit, Michigan. In her words, she was in a "comfortable place" and would have been happy to stay there for a long time. Then the recession hit, with Detroit at the epicenter. Mental healthcare became a luxury people could no longer afford.

Daphne's income dwindled, as fewer and fewer clients came to see her. She prayed and sought God's direction, but felt certain God was telling her that she was doing what He wanted her to do. "It's hard for me to explain how I knew this was God's leading," she shares, "other than to say that I had a confidence or certainty deep inside." Her certainty was of little comfort, though, as her practice continued to decline.

Eventually, Daphne ran out of money and lost her home. It was devastating for her. She couldn't help wondering, "Did I miss something? Did I mistake my wishes for God's direction?" The results certainly pointed in that direction. During this time, Daphne prayed many, "God-what-are-you-doing?" kinds of prayers, but no answers seemed to materialize.

While all of this was happening, Daphne also experienced a growing desire to go into some type of church-based ministry. She began to explore whether this might be a calling from God. First she went to several pastors who knew her, as well as to members of her own church. They affirmed the gifts they saw in Daphne and encouraged her to continue pursuing this path. She then started taking seminary classes, to continue exploring and preparing herself for potential church ministry.

But despite all her sincere and faithful efforts to follow God's leading, things went from bad to worse. She learned that she needed surgery and that it would cost her $7,000 after insurance. "Really God, I don't understand," she prayed. "I am pursuing you. I am being faithful. I'm training to serve you more, and I'm doing it because I thought you wanted me to. So, what are you doing to me?"

Despite all that was going wrong, Daphne never doubted God's presence. Although she didn't understand what God was doing, she trusted that God had His reasons. And in the midst of her struggles, God would send reminders of His presence. One month, when she was $1,400 short of what she needed to pay her bills, the money came from places she least expected, covering all her needs with $100 to spare. However, God's biggest reminder of His presence occurred recently.

Daphne was recovering from surgery and needed a place to live. She couldn't afford to pay both the medical bills and the rent. So Daphne prayed what she called a "crazy prayer." She simply said, "God I need a place to live for free." Within ten days, Daphne was asked to be a house sitter in a furnished, 4,000 square foot home for the next twelve months. God is good.

God has taught Daphne some important lessons. Although they were painful, she now sees how necessary they were. Daphne had become too attached to what the Bible calls "the things of this world." She had been too attached to her lifestyle and realizes that she would have never been willing to let it go if God opened up an opportunity for church ministry.

God has taken her through a time of pruning, cutting away things that were going to keep her from being fruitful for God in the future. More than ever, Daphne believes God is preparing her to serve on the staff of a church. And although that future may not be as "comfortable" as what she once enjoyed, it promises to be more exciting and rewarding.

Now Daphne says, "I'm able to let go and follow God." She realizes that she doesn't need the things that once seemed so important to her. More importantly, she has experienced the faithfulness of God in powerful ways.

As a result of her struggles, Daphne can see how God has changed her. "I'm far less anxious than I used to be," she says quickly. "In fact, in the days when things were far more comfortable for me, I had been prone to panic attacks," she admits. Today, the panic attacks are gone, even though her circumstances are far more uncertain. That is the power of living in God's hand, regardless of the struggles of life.

Daphne is eager to stay connected to Jesus. She has spent the better part of the year studying Isaiah chapter 30. Verse 15 of Isaiah 30 says, "This is what the Sovereign LORD, the Holy One of Israel, says: 'In repentance and rest is your salvation, in quietness and trust is your strength.'" This is a verse Daphne has come to understand not only in her head, but also in her heart, and she has been learning to live her life by its truth.

## Make it Personal

- Have you ever experienced a time when God seemed to be delaying His answers or work in your life? What did you learn about God through that experience? What is Daphne learning through her experience of God's delay in her life?

- In John 11:4, Jesus lets the disciples know that Lazarus's sickness would not end in death. And then He waits two more days before going to be with Lazarus. If you were one of the disciples, what would you be thinking as you watched Jesus, apparently in no hurry to help His friend?

- Read Martha's words to Jesus in John 11:21. What do you imagine the tone of her voice is like? The expression on her face? The feelings in her heart? Even though she accuses Jesus of delaying, what element of faith do you still see in her words?

- How can you learn to trust Jesus today, even when you don't understand what He's doing? Even when He seems to be delaying?

- How has Jesus spoken to you in this devotional time?

## Prayer

Dear Jesus, I know that you are good, all the time – even when I don't understand you. Please give me faith today to wait for you, to trust you, to hope in you. Amen.

# PERPLEXED

## In the Word

Read John 11:1-16 and Isaiah 55:8-9.

The disciples couldn't believe they were going back towards Jerusalem. Not long ago, they had to leave Jerusalem because it was becoming too dangerous. There had been death threats against them. Several times people had tried to stone Jesus. Jerusalem wasn't safe for them, so why was Jesus taking them back there? He said they were going to wake up Lazarus, which didn't make any sense. Then Jesus said that Lazarus was dead, which made even less sense. But even though they didn't understand, they followed Jesus anyway.

Jesus can be confusing at times, doing things that don't make sense or taking us in directions we don't understand. In those moments, can we trust that He sees a bigger picture? That He has a bigger plan? That He knows what He is doing even if we don't like it? That if we go along with Him, we will see God's power at work?

## Mary Shisler's Story

Mary knows all about prayer not being answered the way she expected. Growing up as a pastor's kid, in a strong and loving Christian home, Mary's early life was filled with positive experiences. It was easy for Mary to believe in God and to follow Him. It was easy to believe that God is good and He would always answer her prayers. But as she grew older, Mary's experiences caused her to question those beliefs.

After marrying her high school sweetheart, Mary and Larry went to Bible school and started their family. By the time she was pregnant with their third child, Larry was serving as the pastor of a small church in a California mountain community. Life was still good, but very busy.

In their church and town, there had been a lot of hurt and division over the years. So Mary and Larry began praying that God would unite the people of their small town, but the answer did not come in a way they expected.

One weekend Mary's blood pressure suddenly spiked and she experienced rapid weight gain. She went in to see her doctor and learned that she had preeclampsia a potentially life-threatening condition experienced during some pregnancies. Mary was rushed to the hospital, several hours away, and spent the next four months in bed. The doctors contacted her family and told them she might not live through it.

It was a stressful time for all of them. But this was when God began to answer prayer in an unexpected way. "The whole town came together," Mary remembers. "They helped provide us with meals and even childcare." As people served together, wounds were healed and the town had a total change. "It was the answer to what I was praying – it just wasn't the way I wanted it. God didn't clear his methods with me first."

Finally their third child was born – on Tax Day. "Everything about her birth and that day was taxing," Mary says with a smile. Their daughter was born two months prematurely, and the doctors didn't think she would survive. They whisked her away to the Medical Center at UC Davis, which was several hours away from their home. And there, Mary says, "we learned about life and death on a daily basis."

When their daughter was two weeks old, Mary and Larry met with the four doctors on their daughter's care team. They said, "she most likely will not survive, so you shouldn't get too attached. If she does live, she won't live past the age of three. And even if she does make it past three, she'll never make it past ten." Mary and Larry were devastated.

But after three of the doctors had left the room, a fourth doctor stopped and said, "But you know, we're not God. We really can't tell what's going to happen." This opened the door once again for hope, fueling Mary's prayers. But her faith was being seriously tested for the first time in her life, and God didn't seem to be answering.

They named their daughter Janelle Nicole, because Janelle means "God is gracious," and Nicole means "victorious in strife." And they held onto the hope that she would live up to her name. Finally, when she was three months old, they were able to bring her home. She had many needs – and still does to this day.

Janelle is the reason Mary began spending so much time in God's word. "Much like a starving man doesn't become whole in one meal," she says. "I had to hear again and again about how God is good and He does good things, even when I don't understand. I had to learn that God is still good, even when He says, 'no.'"

Janelle lived at home for sixteen years before they found a wonderful, private-care Christian home that has 24/7 access to medical care. Because of this high level of care, Janelle's health is now much stronger than it was prior to moving there. Even though she has come close to dying numerous times, today she is a strong 27 year-old.

"She's a real kick," says Mary. "Sometimes she's a bit of a rascal, with a sadistic sense of humor." Although Janelle has numerous physical and mental challenges, she is a happy young woman who likes to go to movies and get her nails done. Since her vocal chords were paralyzed at birth, she has developed her own version of sign language that helps her communicate what she wants. "She's a real favorite where she lives, and everyone loves her," Mary says proudly.

Although Mary still has questions about why God allowed this, she can see how God has used Janelle's life for good. "I really thank God for her because she's the one who drove me to the depths of my faith. My experiences with Janelle have taught me how to still be joyful. They have also given me the ability to do what I do on a day-to-day basis, working with special ed. kids in the high school."

There have been many times when they thought they had lost Janelle, "But then suddenly, she would pop right back out of it!" Mary laughs. "My daughter has far out-lived any expectation that was ever had for her. And though it's still heart-wrenching whenever she goes downhill, I have a totally different view of what it will be like when she's finally in heaven. I think about that song 'I Am Free To Run,' and I know that will be true for Janelle. She can't run here on earth, but when she's finally home, she'll be able to run and she'll finally be able to talk. It's exciting," says Mary.

"I know that God loves her much more than even I do. Even though I still don't understand everything, I know that He knit her together in my womb and her life is in His hands."

## Make it Personal

- In today's story, Mary didn't understand why God didn't answer her prayers the way she wanted, and why He allowed Janelle to have so many struggles. What would you say to Mary about that if you could talk to her? In what ways was God good to Mary, even in the midst of the challenges?

- Why do you suppose God doesn't always explain what He's doing in our lives or why He's doing it? How does God change us as we follow Him anyway, even when we don't understand?

- Read Isaiah 55:8-9 and consider how God's ways are higher than your ways. How have you seen this to be true in your own life? In the lives of others?

- How has Jesus spoken to you in this devotional time?

## Prayer

Dear Jesus, I don't always understand you. But you tell me I don't have to understand in order to believe. You simply invite me to follow and trust you. Please help me to do that today, no matter what the day may bring. Amen.

# RESTORATION

## In the Word

Read John 11:38-44 and Ephesians 3:20-21.

Martha was struggling to believe. When Jesus said, "I am the resurrection and the life," she told Jesus that she believed, but it turns out there were limits to her belief. Martha simply could not comprehend the full implications of Jesus being the resurrection and the life. It was beyond what she could imagine.

Sometimes we have trouble imagining a resurrection in our own lives. "It's too late" we believe. "The habit is too strong." "The wounds are too many." "The situation has gone on for too long." We can believe the same things about a friend. We wish for a resurrection in their lives, but find it hard to believe it could happen, "They're too far gone."

Jesus said, "I am the resurrection and the life. Did I not tell you that if you believed, you would see the glory of God?

## Amy Ayer's Story

She could see the semi-truck heading toward her, and in desperation she thought, "I should just drive into that truck." It's hard for Amy to believe that was just a few years ago. "I was so broken," she remembers, "that I didn't want to be alive."

Amy's pain actually began at an early age. When she was only eight years old, Amy made the decision that she was on her own. Growing up in an alcoholic family, home life was crazy and loud. One night her father dragged her out of bed, screaming at her and her mother. That's when she saw the pills in her mother's hand, and could see that her mother wanted to take them. "Mom was always the one that made me feel safe and cared for," Amy explains. "And I realized at that point that she could be gone at any time. So I decided that I was on my own."

Amy spent her growing up years learning to fend for herself, and looking for relationships that would help her not feel so alone. Eventually she married a man who seemed like a healthy person, and they began their life together. But during their years together, she learned that what you see on the outside of a person isn't necessarily what's going on inside.

Their marriage ended in an ugly divorce. "I was filled with rage, hurt, and fear," she says. "I'd never been so afraid in all my life. I had no way of financially supporting myself because I had been a stay-at-home mom." At that time in her life, Amy remembers not having a strong enough sense of self to fight for anything, so she left the marriage with nothing. "Everything was removed from me. All the things you think make you look normal, the house, the dog, even the landscaping in the backyard, it was all gone just like that. All I had was my car, my guitar, and the kids."

This began what Amy calls the "Restoration Amy Project." At that time, she knew about God, but He wasn't a priority in her life. "God was in my life," she explains, "but He wasn't my life." Yet looking back now, it's clear to Amy that God was at work.

"God provided for me in the most ridiculous ways," she smiles. And He kept her from acting on her impulse to drive into oncoming trucks. She began listening to some Joyce Meyer CD's that a friend had given her. As she drove each day, she would try to tune out the ugly thoughts that filled her mind, and focus instead on the truth she was hearing on the CD.

"Finally I made a decision," Amy remembers. "I said, 'God, I've made a mess of my life. I don't want to live anymore. But I'm going to give you one shot. I'm going to give you *all* of me – everything. You are going to *be* my life. And if I do that, would you show me that my life is worth living?"

With tears of gratitude, Amy says, "He came and restored every area of my life. I am a testimony of His victory. He restored me. He healed me. He gave me scripture. He gave me people who could explain scripture.

Sometimes He just came into my heart to show me things."

It's been five years since she gave her heart to Christ, and she's still on a journey with Him. She jokes about wanting to wear a t-shirt that says, "Please Be Patient, God Is Not Finished With Me Yet," because every day she can see ways that He is still shaping her character and changing her heart. Amy continues to learn that she should never take over the wheel of her own life – she needs to keep giving control to God.

Amy describes herself as being hungry for God, and now that she is remarried to a wonderful Christian man, she's hungry to learn how to be a godly wife. She's also hungry to learn how to be a godly parent. "I'm hungry every day," she says. "And God is with me every day. I wake up in the morning and He's with me. I go to work and He's with me. I come home and He's with me. That's how this whole transformation thing is working. It's out of being really hungry."

And she's learning to obey Him, even if He asks her to do things that are outside of her comfort zone. For example, she knew God was leading her to go to church. But this was hard for her, because people at church all looked so good and "put together." She didn't feel like she fit in. She was afraid of looking stupid or being rejected. "But He taught me to keep coming to church even if I didn't feel like it," she says. "He told me to just be vulnerable and humble, and that's what I did."

"I just did what He asked me to do," she explains, "because I was so completely confident that I had no other alternative but to listen to Him." And Amy's heart to listen and obey is bringing amazing fruit in her life. She's learning that she can trust God, that He is faithful, and that He can do a much better job with her life than she ever could.

Best of all, she's learning that in Christ she is a new creation. "I don't have to feel ashamed about where I came from. I don't have to feel 'less than' because I came from a home that only looked normal. I don't have to be ashamed that my bad marriage fell apart. I don't have to feel any of those things because here's the deal – you get to start over with God! With Christ, you get do-overs."

As she is being restored, she is also learning how important it is to stay close to Christ. She can see that the devil uses so many means to try and discourage her and separate her from God. "His goal is to make you feel like you don't belong when you walk into church. It's a real battle out there." Which is why Amy says it's so important to "keep the vehicle ready." Keeping the vehicle of her life ready involves ongoing maintenance. Things like studying God's word, serving others and staying connected with other believers.

Even though she felt like she was on her own as a little girl, Amy now knows that she is never alone. Instead, she is discovering that when she steps out in faith, God is always there to catch her.

## Make it Personal

- In today's story, how did Amy experience the truth of Ephesians 3:20-21? In what ways did she experience what Lazarus did? How can you relate to her story?

- In John 11:39, Martha raises an objection to Jesus' request. Like Martha, have you ever experienced a time when you felt the need to help God understand why His request is not a good idea?

- Rather than focusing on the smelly tomb, what does Jesus focus on when he responds to Martha's objection? What can we learn from this about where our focus should be?

- After Lazarus comes out of the tomb, he is still wrapped in grave clothes. Jesus tells them to unbind him and let him go. How does this give us a picture of the role of the church in the lives of people? In what ways can we help remove people's grave clothes?

- How has Jesus spoken to you in this devotional time?

## Prayer

Dear Jesus, you *are* the resurrection and the life. Please pour your life into me today and resurrect the dead places within me. Help me to hold on to the truth and the hope that you are able to do far more than I could ever ask or imagine. I praise you for that! Amen.

# CHANGE of HEART

## In the Word

Read John 11:25-27 and Mark 10:26-27.

It really comes down to that one simple question: "Do you believe this?" Do you believe that Jesus *will* make a difference in your life? For five weeks, you have been reading the testimonies of people whose lives have been changed by Jesus. These stories aren't made up, they all really happened.

Jesus does make a difference! He can and will resurrect the dead or dying parts of your life. He's proven it over and over. Will you let him? Do you believe this?

## Cathie's Story

Cathie was angry at God. She had grown up in church, but she was ANGRY. Just before her fourteenth birthday, her dad was killed by a drunk driver. "Why was such a good man taken away, while the guilty man survives?" she demanded of God. Cathie's mom tried to hold it together so she could take care of Cathie and her baby sister, but it was a struggle. Understandably, she was devastated by the sudden loss of the man she loved and counted on. Meanwhile, Cathie found herself not only dealing with the loss of her father, but also thrust into the role of trying to support her mom.

With dad gone and God rejected in anger, Cathie went into her high school years feeling a void of love. Like so many teenage girls before and after her, she turned to guys to fill the void. "Before I finished high school, I was pregnant and married, in that order," she shares. "We were kids having a fling, and now we were trying to be adults before we were ready."

Cathie's husband was into drinking and drugs, and soon Cathie was joining him. Her husband was also into womanizing. He was still a kid after all, but that didn't go over well. Somehow the marriage lasted ten years and produced a son and a daughter before they divorced.

Still reeling from the pain of her broken marriage, Cathie soon met and married another guy. Sadly, this guy wasn't an improvement. He also drank and used drugs, but then again, so did Cathie. There was a new twist, however; although her husband initially showered Cathie with attention, soon after they were married, he turned violent. But Cathie, the classic victim, stayed with him until she finally hit bottom.

"One day when I came home and called for my son, there was no answer," she remembers. "He should have been home from high school at that time. So I called again – nothing. I went up to his room to find him, and when I opened the door I found…nothing. The room was completely cleaned out. My son had packed up all his belongings and left without any warning to go live with his dad." Cathie's son was fed up with the drinking, drugs and violence in the house.

That was the breaking point, the wake up call Cathie needed. It was August 1984, and Cathie still vividly remembers going into her darkened bedroom and sobbing. In the midst of her tears, she realized she needed Jesus in her life. She cried out that famous prayer of desperation: "Jesus, please get me out of this mess I've made of my life, and I'll do anything you want. I'll serve you the rest of my life!" The difference between her prayers and the prayers of so many others, is that Cathie truly meant what she said. Soon, she was the one packing up her stuff and escaping the house with her young daughter.

Cathie began turning her life around. She poured herself into reading the Bible and began to experience Jesus' presence giving her the strength to quit drugs and drinking. Cathie found herself becoming a new woman, a healed woman, a woman who was loved by God.

As Cathie followed Jesus, her life was turned around. First, she met a good man, Hank, and they have been happily married for 25 years. Next, Jesus gave Cathie a purpose. She became involved with prison ministry. She found she could relate to the female inmates because she knew that before finding Jesus she could easily have landed in jail herself. Through the prison ministry Cathie counseled inmates, led Sunday morning church services, and even helped some get into Christian transitional programs after they were released.

Cathie also began working with addicts and the homeless. "I could tell that God had made a difference in my life," she says, "when I found myself truly caring for a homeless alcoholic living under a highway overpass. This woman admitted to me that she had killed several people through drunk driving – the same thing that had killed my own father and sent my life into a tailspin." With Cathie's help, and the help of other Christians, this woman is no longer drinking, has a job, and is functioning in society once again.

Cathie's son and daughter have also both become Christians. Her daughter accepted Christ as a child, but her son didn't become a Christian until he was well into his adult years – and not until he had hit bottom on his own self-destructive path of drugs and alcohol. At that point, much like Cathie did, he knew he needed a Savior, so he called on Jesus to rescue him.

A few years ago they attended the funeral of their dad, Cathie's first husband. Neither he, nor Cathie's second husband, ever left their partying ways. Both died by the time they were sixty, victims of their wasted lives of alcohol and drugs.

After the funeral, Cathie's daughter reminisced on what life might have been like for all of them if Cathie had not cried out to Jesus that August night in 1984. They smiled together as they realized what a difference Jesus has made in Cathie's life, which in turn changed her kids' lives, and is now blessing her grandkids' lives.

## Make it Personal

- Like many people, Cathie had to hit bottom before she was ready to believe in Jesus. In what ways can you relate to this story? Where are you on your journey of faith in Jesus?

- To believe or have faith means having a trust that leads to action. In what ways did Cathie act on her belief, rather than simply saying the words, "I believe"?

- Read Mark 10:26-27 again, but this time continue on and read verse 28 as well. What evidence of belief do you see in the disciples? What evidence of belief do you see in the people involved in the Lazarus story of John 11? If someone were to look at your life, what evidence of belief would they see?

- How might you be finding it difficult to believe today? Why is that? How is Jesus asking you step out in faith, even though it may be hard?

- How has Jesus spoken to you in this devotional time?

## Prayer

Dear Jesus, I do believe. Please help me with my unbelief. I recognize that faith is an action word. Give me the courage to act on my faith today, trusting that you are God and you are in control. Amen.

# WITNESS

## In the Word

Read John 12:9-11, Acts 1:7-8 and Matthew 5:14-16.

Jesus is the resurrection and the life. That is great news! Jesus can fill people's deepest needs and transform their lives. He makes a real difference. Do you believe this? Do you believe that Jesus is the solution to the struggles that people around you are having? Do you believe He can change lives?

How has Jesus changed your life? There's power in the story of God's work in your life. Be a witness to that resurrection today, and tell people what Jesus has done for you – and what you know Jesus can do for them.

## Lisa Thompson's Story

Lisa never thought of herself as an evangelist – that was a word to describe people like Billy Graham or Luis Palau, people with an obvious gift for public speaking and leading people to faith in Christ. But about twelve years ago, God began breaking Lisa's heart for the needs of all the moms she was getting to know through her kids' school. Lisa soon discovered that when God gets hold of your heart, you can't ignore it. She found her burden for these women weighing heavily on her, night and day.

"After lots of prodding and my heart changing," says Lisa, "I knew it was time to step out and minister to women who didn't have the hope I have, the resources I have, the understanding of scripture I have. I kept thinking that if they only knew what I know and *who* I know, it would completely change their life."

Lisa could see that the struggles these women had were much the same as any of her own struggles. They had challenges in their marriages, in their parenting, and in how they see themselves in the mirror. The difference was that "I went to bed at night knowing that God was going to take care of it for me," Lisa says. "They didn't have that."

So, feeling very unqualified for the task, Lisa gathered a group of eighteen unchurched women and began a home Bible study. "All I did," she explains, "is say yes to God. It was a response of obedience." Leading a group like this was completely outside of Lisa's comfort zone. In her experience, "women can be so guarded, and there's so much pain and insecurity to break through." But as she met faithfully with these women week after week, she began to see amazing fruit.

Lisa saw women deciding to follow Jesus and she watched how it began to bring healing into their lives and marriages and homes. She saw women grow in fellowship with one another and provide an open, accepting environment to explore their questions about God and the Bible. But perhaps most surprising of all was the fruit Lisa began to see in her own life.

Before starting this study, from the world's perspective, Lisa had it all – the home, the marriage, the kids, the money in the bank, and physically being in the best shape of her life. But as she began to step out to lead, serve, and love these women, God began to change her priorities. Material comfort was no longer a priority. And appearing to have it all together was also no longer a priority.

The women of Lisa's "Faith Journey" Bible study group tell her how much they have enjoyed watching her change over the years. The biggest change they have seen – and the biggest change Lisa has experienced – is the freedom she feels to be completely authentic. She doesn't worry so much about being a people pleaser. She doesn't worry about any of her weaknesses or flaws because, as she's learned, "God can still use it all for His purposes."

The more freed up she is to truly be herself, the more powerful her testimony is with women who need Jesus. "This freedom is allowing women to see more of Christ and less of Lisa," she explains. It's not always comfortable, and it's definitely been humbling, but she wouldn't trade the joy she's experienced for anything in the world.

Just last year, God allowed Lisa to watch God unfold a miracle in one family. She met a woman who was struggling in the parenting of her teenage daughter. She was at her wits end. So Lisa invited her to the small group Bible study, and Lisa was thrilled to watch this woman's faith – and parenting – grow stronger. Lisa encouraged her to sign her daughter up for a mission trip to Mexico that the teens from Lisa's church were going on over spring break. Reluctantly, this rebellious teen signed up and went to the first training meeting – and she LOVED it. "The daughter began to be completely changed – even before going to Mexico," Lisa shares, "just as a result of going to the training meetings."

Lisa was privileged to go on that trip as an adult leader, and this young girl was in Lisa's group. According to Lisa, this girl "has Jesus written on the outside of her. A lot of kids keep their Jesus inside, but this girl – it's all over her." And now the entire family is being transformed and are coming regularly to church together.

Over the years, Faith Journey Bible Study has continued to grow. Now there are multiple women helping to lead in multiple locations. Lisa continues to see unchurched women attending and growing, and eventually getting plugged into local churches. In addition, God has inspired Lisa to write the curriculum they use each year, developing an in-depth approach to scripture that is user-friendly for spiritual seekers.

So, does Lisa see herself as an evangelist now? Absolutely. In fact, "we're all called to evangelize and profess the hope that we believe," she shares. "We each do it differently, with our different gifts and voices and spheres of influence." But Lisa sees now that our greatest evangelism comes without even using words.

"It's the way we love Jesus Christ. That is what the world is drawn to," she says. "They're not drawn to how much scripture we've memorized or how we communicate – that's not really impressive. They're drawn to Jesus when we're broken and don't have it all together. And when they watch us walk through difficult things and yet they see the rock on which we stand –

that's a huge testimony."

Lisa is a witness to the resurrection. She experienced the difference Jesus' presence makes in her life, and was confident that Jesus could make a difference in other women's lives. By saying yes to God and being a witness, countless lives and entire families have been transformed.

## Make it Personal

- Do you see yourself as an evangelist? In what ways does that term perhaps intimidate you? What do you learn about evangelism from Lisa's story? How might you follow her example?

- What would it look like for you to "shine" for Jesus today?

- How do you think Lazarus' experience with Jesus changed him? What do you imagine he would tell people about his experience?

- In what ways has Jesus changed you? How can you let Him use your experiences with Him to be a witness to others?

- In Acts 1:7-8, Jesus tells the disciples that they will receive the Holy Spirit in order to be witnesses throughout the world. When you finish this "I AM" series, you may want to read the entire book of Acts to see how God used a rag tag group of followers to make an impact on the entire world. What difference does it make to you, knowing that the Holy Spirit is available to help you share the Good News?

- How has Jesus spoken to you in this devotional time?

## Prayer

Dear Jesus, your resurrection is truly good news! Please help me not to keep that good news to myself, but to freely share it with others, letting your light shine through me today. Amen.

a spiritual practice
# KEEPING THE SABBATH

Keeping the Sabbath is a way we can experience the resurrection life of Jesus in our own lives. The goal of Sabbath is to take a day completely off from any kind of labor to enjoy the blessings of God. It takes trust in God to actually do this, but when you do, God's presence will rejuvenate you.

**Imagine Following Your Bliss**
Consider making today a day of Sabbath (or plan to take a Sabbath within the next few days). Sabbath is a day free of anything that feels like work, so that you can enjoy the goodness of God.

Imagine what it would feel like to wake up on a Sabbath day and know that you are completely free to follow your bliss. Imagine being able to rest, play and be with the ones you love in ways that are different from other days. Imagine feeling relaxed and at peace. This is just a fraction of what Sabbath is about, but it is a beginning.

Take time to think through the preparations you will need to make so that you can be truly free to enjoy the Sabbath. Is there food to be bought and prepared ahead? Is there cleaning or errands that need to be completed? What kinds of changes will need to be made in the other six days of your week in order to make room for Sabbath?

In the Old Testament, Sabbath was always celebrated in the context of family and loved ones. So talk about the Sabbath with your family, and come up with ideas of what you can do together to enjoy the Sabbath.

**Possible Sabbath Activities**
The idea behind Sabbath is to set aside time for intimacy with God and those you love – it's a time to rest and recover from the busyness of the week. Depending on what kinds of activities rejuvenate you the most,

consider one or more of the following ways to spend your Sabbath:

- Playing games with the family
- Going for a relaxed walk
- Taking a nap
- Reading a good book
- Reading THE Good Book (i.e. the Bible)
- Going for a picnic
- Making a phone call to someone you love
- Having tea or coffee with a friend
- Making love with your spouse
- Doing something creative like playing the piano or painting a picture

On your Sabbath, you may also want to consider:

- Avoiding activities that cause you stress
- Saving difficult conversations for another day
- Refraining from making a "to-do" list
- Refraining from competition that moves you into a bad place

**The Purpose of Sabbath**

The Sabbath teaches us to trust God. Often we overwork because we fear that if we don't, we'll fail and not be able to provide for ourselves and our family. God knew we would struggle with this, so He included keeping the Sabbath as one of the Ten Commandments. Keeping the Sabbath, then, becomes a concrete way in which we exercise our trust in God and experience His faithfulness to provide for us.

Sabbath is a way of honoring our God-given limits and caring for ourselves – body, mind, and soul. It is a way of delighting in God's good gifts and slowing down enough to truly savor them. And it is a time to trust God with all the tasks that remain undone.

**When to Keep the Sabbath**

In the Jewish tradition, Sabbath was celebrated on Saturday. However, after Christ rose from the dead on a Sunday, Christians began celebrating the Sabbath on Sundays. It really doesn't matter which day of the week you observe Sabbath; what is important is that we follow God's instructions and have a Sabbath, a day of rest, once a week.

# Week 6

# "I Am the Way, the Truth, and the Life"

The room was quiet, the feeling was unsettled. They were all gathered for the Passover meal. The meal was a solemn ritual that was celebrated every year to remember the night God set their ancestors free from their bondage in Egypt. On that night, God instructed all the Israelites to smear the blood of a sacrificed lamb on their doorposts. The blood would save them from a curse of death that God was going to bring on all the first-born of the land.

That event was now commemorated every year with the Passover meal. The meal had a formal ritual, with a set script of words that had been done the same way for centuries. But Jesus surprised them when he changed the script.

"This is *my body* given for you; do this in remembrance of me," Jesus said as he broke the unleavened bread and began to pass it around. "This cup is the new covenant in *my blood*, which is poured out for you," he said over the cup of blessing at the end of the meal. Those were eerie words. The disciples began exchanging worried glances back and forth.

Then there was the tense exchange Jesus had with Judas during the meal. Judas had left and never returned. That, too, was confusing and added to everyone's uneasiness.

After the meal Jesus began teaching. "I go to prepare a place for you...I will come back and take you to be with me...You know the way to the place I am going."

Thomas' confusion had reached its breaking point. He blurted out, "Lord, we don't know where you're going, so how can we know the way to get there?"

Another way to put it would be, "Show us the way!"

That's a question men and women have been asking forever. "What is the way that will bring me happiness?" "What is the way that will fulfill me?" "What is the way that will make me secure?" "What is the way to discovering the truth?" "What is the way to really living life?" "What is the way to God?"

Those are life questions. We have all asked some variation of those questions at one time or another. And there is an answer.

Jesus answered Thomas' question with what may be His most controversial I AM statement. *"I am the way and the truth and the life. No one comes to the Father except through me."*

# PURPOSE

## In the Word

Read John 14:1-6 and Ephesians 2:10.

You know that feeling of being lost? It's not a good feeling. Most people, maybe all people, hate being lost. We especially hate being lost in life. When we don't have a purpose or direction, life becomes meaningless, "a chasing after the wind," Solomon calls it in the book of Ecclesiastes.

Having a purpose is one of our deepest needs. We all have a desire to be significant in some way. In this world, there are a lot of "ways" people follow as they seek purpose and meaning. Are they all equally valid – or is there a true way?

Jesus proclaimed that He is the true way. He has a purpose and design for our lives, and His Presence will not only reveal our purpose, but give us the power to accomplish it.

## Taylor Harmon's Story

Just like many sixteen-year-olds, Taylor enjoys going to the mall and hanging out with friends. But unlike many other teens, or even adults for that matter, she knows her purpose in life – it's to use her gifts to honor God and help others know Him.

This past summer, Taylor began to see that God might be calling her to use her love of talking to become a Christian speaker and teacher. While serving as a summer intern at her church, she was asked to lead daily devotionals for the summer ministry team. She was excited by the opportunity because that's exactly what she had been asking God to allow her to do.

"I love communicating and putting things into words," she says. "And I really love talking about God. So that was hitting my sweet spot." Throughout the summer, Taylor had a number of adult leaders confirm to her that she has a real gift in this area and that she should continue to use it. "It was like a big handshake from God," she says, "telling me to keep going, that I'm on the right path."

At one point in the summer, the interns took a trip to work with the homeless in Santa Cruz. While they were there, the team leaders asked for volunteers to give their testimony. At first Taylor resisted this invitation because she felt she had already been up in front of everyone so often.

That's when she flipped her Bible open and her eyes landed on I Peter 4:10-11 where it says, "Each of you should use whatever gift you have received to serve others... If anyone speaks, they should do so as one who speaks the very words of God." She took it as a sign from God, encouraging her to step out again and share.

So once again Taylor put her growing gift of public speaking into use. After sharing her faith story and encouraging the homeless people from scripture, she gave an altar call. Three homeless men raised their hand, indicating that they wanted to accept Christ.

"It was the coolest feeling," Taylor shares. "I think this may be what God wants me to do for the rest of my life. Maybe not – but I hope so. I love it when the Holy Spirit moves through me and talks through me."

Taylor's experience is a great example of how God gives each of us gifts, and when we use them the way He desires, our lives have direction, purpose and joy. Taylor is also a great reminder that it doesn't matter what your age is, you're never too young or too old to find God's direction.

But Taylor didn't always have a clear sense of God's direction in her life. And she didn't always want to share her faith. For many years, ballet was the most important thing in her life. She danced every day – as many as fourteen hours a week. During those years, God was part of her life, but He wasn't her top priority.

During her junior high years in particular, she was still active in her church, but she admits, "I was just faking it, trying to put on a Christian face." And during her sixth grade year, when her uncle unexpectedly died, she began to question everything about God.

At that time, dancing was center stage in Taylor's life, even though it often caused her great pain. Her dance instructor was a very strict ballet master who spoke French and would tap the ground with his yardstick when he was unhappy with her – often speaking rudely to her and the other girls.

Sometimes, she remembers, he would tap her on the stomach and say, "too fat, too fat." Taylor was shocked, and wounded. "If I think back to when my self-esteem began to be destroyed, that was the breaking point," she says. "In ballet, you're in tights and a leotard in front of a mirror, with plenty of girls to compare yourself to." At that point, Taylor began to tell herself, "You're too ugly for this. You're not good enough. You can't do this. All these girls are better than you."

Taylor is so thankful that throughout those years God put many godly mentors into her life, including her parents, to counterbalance the negative messages she was hearing and starting to believe. Then, before her sophomore year in high school, she spent several weeks in Mississippi at a Christian ballet camp called, "Ballet Magnificat." That was the summer God began to heal Taylor's heart and show her that her life has purpose.

"I learned that God wants me to dance for Him in *every* ballet class, not just the Christian ones. And God wants me to praise Him with everything I have," says Taylor. "That summer I had a lot of truth spoken into my life about who I am, my self-image, and how God created me for a reason."

Taylor continues to dance, but ballet is no longer what defines who she is – her life purpose is all about pursuing Jesus. Taylor is passionate about sharing the messages He's given her, saying that, "Life is short and we need to make whatever impact we can. God put us here on earth for a reason, and we need to figure out what that is and then live each day sharing God's love with everyone around us."

She also gets animated when she shares what she wants other teenagers to know. "I want them to know they don't have to fix their lives before they come to Jesus," she says. "He wants you to come to Him with your burdens and let Him meet those needs." Taylor sees so many teens looking for love and acceptance in all the wrong places. "But really, the only thing that can fill that hole inside is Christ. God's love is so constant," she shares. "I think that's so amazing, because in a teenager's life, things are such a roller coaster of emotions. Like, today we're dating, and tomorrow we're not dating. But it's so different with God. He doesn't ever change."

It looks like Taylor will be one to watch in the years to come as she lets God use her in big ways.

## Make it Personal

- As Taylor steps out and uses her gifts, she is discovering more of God's purpose for her life. In what ways are you discovering God's purpose for your life? Who might help you discern God's purpose? What steps can you take today to explore and pursue your purpose?

- Ephesians 2:10 says that you are God's "workmanship, created in Christ Jesus to do good works." The word workmanship has the meaning of exquisite craftsmanship. What does it mean to you that you are exquisitely made? In what ways has God crafted you and given you unique gifts to share with the world?

- Read John 14:1-6 again. What grabs your attention about Jesus' words here to the disciples? What is comforting about His words? What is challenging?

- As it says in the opening of today's devotional, there are many "ways" that people follow. What are some of the ways you've seen? What are some ways that you have followed? What are some of the differences between those "ways" and Jesus as *the* Way?

- How has Jesus spoken to you in this devotional time?

## Prayer

Dear Jesus, thank you for being *the* Way and providing direction for our lives. Help me to continue walking with you by faith, following your way for my life. Help me to discover more of your purpose for my life and to live it out. Amen.

# FINDING YOUR WAY

## In the Word

Read Matthew 6:31-33, Psalm 37:4, and John 6:66-69.

You may have a "way" you're following, but you're still lost if it's the wrong way. Some people try to go the way of business success. Others choose popularity. Some are hedonists. People also pursue different ways when seeking spiritual truth. Some try various religious paths. Others live as practical atheists. Most end up asking, "Is this all there is?"

Jesus declares another way, a true way that leads to life. This way is surprising because it's not a cause or a profession. Jesus says the true way is a person – Him. Our purpose is to believe in Him, love Him, follow Him and honor Him. When we are focused on Him, we end up finding the way that ignites our passion and gives us purpose and meaning.

After you make the commitment to follow Jesus, start paying attention to the leanings of your heart. You may discover that Jesus is using them to nudge you towards your God-given purpose.

## Gary Downing's Story

Gary lounged on the beach, enjoying the sun, the Gulf breeze and the girls walking by. He was living the dream. As a high school student, he had always dreamed of becoming a fighter pilot. Now he was on his way. He was a midshipman at the United States Naval Academy, assigned for the summer to the Pensacola Naval Air Station to receive flight indoctrination. Days in the sky, evenings at the Officer's Club, and weekends on the beach

– life couldn't be better. But something didn't quite feel right.

"I recall thinking that my life was like a red balloon," Gary says. "I was shiny on the outside, but inside I was nothing but hot air." Although he was achieving his dream, he wondered, "Is this as good as it gets?"

One weekend he and a friend decided to stop at church on their way to the beach. They were Christians after all, so going to church seemed like the right thing to do. It also seemed like a good place to meet some girls and invite them to the beach.

You never know when or where God is going to get your attention. Gary went to church to look for girls, not hear from God, but it was God who got his attention. Something hit him hard during that service. Afterwards, he gave the car keys to his friend and asked him to pick him up later that evening. Gary needed some time alone to do some thinking.

Hour after hour, Gary walked the beach. He barely noticed the beauty of his surroundings – the glistening white sand, the pelicans diving for fish, or the flashes of sunlight reflecting off the Gulf waters. He didn't even pay attention to the sunbathing girls who were checking him out. He was wrestling with God.

Years before, as a second grade boy at summer camp, Gary remembered feeling God calling him to be a pastor. But he was only eight years old. It was just the imagination of a young boy. Right? Gary had long since abandoned those thoughts to pursue his real passion of being a fighter pilot. But he had never forgotten that summer camp experience, and now it was all coming back, haunting him.

"Flying is what I want to do," Gary argued with God. "It's been my singular desire and passion for years." But even as he said it, Gary realized that something was missing. He didn't feel as fulfilled as he expected. It seemed that God was telling Gary that He had different plans for him, a different profession. But that didn't make any sense.

He was in the Naval Academy, one of the elite few on the path towards becoming a fighter pilot. That's not something you just walk away from. "I would be letting my parents down," he argued. "They are so proud of me. And I'd be abandoning my dream. For what? To be a pastor? God you have got to be kidding! Plus, what if I did quit? What would I do then? I don't have any money. I don't have the resources to pursue anything else."

· Gary spent hours piling on the arguments, but as he did, this question kept piercing his thoughts: "Is flying going to be your god, or am I going to be your God?"

Gary finally turned and watched as the sunset turned the ocean a deep red. As he watched the beauty unfold, he was struck with a realization. The God who made this vast ocean could easily provide the resources he would need to change course in his life. With the skies now darkening, Gary continued to walk down the beach. He had made his decision. He was surrendering himself to God's direction. He would leave the Naval Academy and the dream of being a fighter pilot in order to become a pastor. It sounded crazy.

As he walked along the beach, he prayed, "God this doesn't make sense to me. I don't know where this is going to lead, but I'm going to trust you." He then looked down at his footprints. They were glowing from the red phosphorous in the sand. For Gary, it was God's little way of saying, "I am going to be with you every step of the way."

When Gary called home to tell his dad of his decision, he braced himself for the reaction, but it was worse than he expected. His dad started weeping on the phone. "Oh wow," Gary thought, "I've really hurt him." Then his dad choked back his tears and said, "Son, your mom and I have been praying for this for the past two years."

When Gary left the Naval Academy he didn't know what was going to happen next. He was starting over. But within ten days he was accepted to a new college and given a job and a place to live. God already had everything lined up. He was just waiting on Gary to catch up.

In college, Gary discovered a ministry called Young Life. As he worked with kids, he discovered his God-given passion. He continued on as a Young Life staff worker after college and ministered to kids for years. He eventually moved on to teaching youth leadership courses in seminary, training the next generation of youth leaders, as well as spending the next twenty years serving as a pastor.

It was supposed to have been a quick stop at a church to "check-in" with God, but instead, Gary found his purpose in life. That purpose transformed his selfish emptiness to rich fullness. When asked if he ever regrets his decision to abandon his dream of being a fighter pilot, Gary is quick to say, "Not even for a moment."

## Make it Personal

- Have you ever had an experience like Gary's, where your life was heading in one direction, but you began to feel led to go in a different direction? What did you do? How was God involved in this?

- When Jesus said, "I am *the* way," He was making perhaps one of His most controversial statements. Can there really be only one way? How do you react to His statement? What right did He have to make this claim?

- What specific instructions does Jesus give in Matthew 6:31-33 about what it means to follow Him, the Way? How can you put those instructions into practice today?

- Psalm 37:4 invites us to take delight in God, and when we do, God will place His desires in our hearts. *Desiring* God and His ways is an important key to following Jesus, the Way. How can you delight in God today? What desires might He be placing on your heart? How might God want you to act on those God-given desires?

- In John 6:68, Peter makes a profession of faith, underscoring that there's no other way than Jesus. What sacrifices might you be called to make in order to live out a similar profession of faith?

- How has Jesus spoken to you in this devotional time?

## Prayer

Dear Jesus, help me keep my eyes on you alone. You are the source of my purpose, direction, and meaning in life. Help me not to seek those things in other places. Today, give me more of a heart to desire you and your ways. Amen.

# WALK the TALK

## In the Word

Read Psalm 14, Proverbs: 11:3, Jeremiah 5:1, and John 8:31-32.

Integrity – it's a word often used and seldom practiced. Jeremiah could not even find one honest man. But truth is a powerful tool in God's toolbox. When we embrace truth, we embrace Jesus who *is* the truth. His truth guides us to right decisions. It brings sin out into the open so we can be set free. It builds rock solid character. It allows us to make a difference. It unleashes God's power in our lives. There are times when the truth will be embarrassing, inconvenient, or painful, but the risk is worth the reward.

## Dave Wertheim's Story

Dave had beads of perspiration forming on his brow. What was he going to do? He was a marketing director for a large technology company and part of a team preparing to launch a new product. At that moment he was sitting in a room full of vice-presidents. They had just handed him a carefully crafted script extolling the virtues of the new product. They expected him to pass it on to his sales force to use when they met with their clients. But there was a problem. Dave knew that as good as the product was, it couldn't live up to the hype of the script.

His mind was racing. "Am I willing to stick to the script and lie for the company? Am I willing to lie to keep my career on track? I could be unemployed by tomorrow. How do you say no to a vice-president?"

Then another thought came into Dave's mind. "Do you love me enough to obey my commands?" Dave took a deep breath and said, "I can't use this." He hoped his voice didn't give away his fear. He suddenly felt like a tasty morsel in a tank full of sharks.

While the executives glared, Dave did his best to explain how the script would misrepresent the product to their customers. No one looked happy. Vice-presidents don't like being told no. They sent him out of the room and Dave feared the worst.

The next day, Dave was asked to meet with the VPs again. He was certain it was to be told that he was fired. When Dave arrived and took a seat, one of the vice-presidents spoke up. "Dave, we apologize for putting you in such an awkward position yesterday. We didn't realize that the script over-exaggerated the product's qualities. The last thing we want to do is to deceive our customers. Thank you for bringing it to our attention. Now, what can we do about it?"

"What!" Dave thought, "Did they just apologize? And now they are asking me for help?" The next thing he knew, Dave had been given complete control over marketing the product. What Dave thought was going to be a career-ender turned into a career-enhancer. That was a powerful lesson for Dave about honoring God by telling the truth. But God has taught Dave that integrity means more than just telling the truth, it also means living the truth.

Dave was always a conscientious and hard working employee, but he wasn't always considerate of others. There were too many times when Dave would ridicule a coworker or brusquely cut them off and dismiss their ideas. But then he would sense Jesus' presence and realize he had failed to bring glory to God.

In these situations, Dave knew he needed to apologize, but he didn't want to. He would argue with God. "It wasn't that bad." "They had it coming." "If I hadn't cut them off we would have wasted too much time." But finally, he would admit the real truth, "I don't like apologizing. It makes me look bad."

Then God would bring one of Dave's favorite Bible verses to mind, Colossians 3:17, which says, "…whatever you do, whether in word or deed, do it all in the name of the Lord Jesus." With that God-given reminder,

Dave would apologize to the people he had treated rudely.

Over time, as Dave sought to have godly integrity in the way he treated others, his character was transformed. He started developing a reputation for being different than most. He had become more sensitive and encouraging. He listened better. He cared for people. After all, how many people voluntarily apologize for slighting others?

Dave says "I seldom tell people at work that I am a Christian. I don't have to. They figure it out." Because his coworkers know that Dave cares, people come to him seeking advice for personal struggles. This has opened up countless doors of opportunity for Dave to naturally talk to people about the difference Jesus has made in his life and can make in theirs as well.

Probably the most difficult, but also the most rewarding lesson Dave learned about integrity happened at a Promise Keepers event. Dave, as one of the leaders in the men's ministry at his church, was there with a large group of men from his church.

The speaker had just finished calling on men who had not been walking with Jesus to come forward and boldly proclaim to everyone that they were going to be committed to following Christ. Hundreds of men came streaming out of the stands to go forward, including a number of men from Dave's own group. Dave was excited and clapped in support. "Good for them for being so bold and committed," he thought.

Then the speaker turned the tables. He said there were men in the arena hiding a secret that poisoned their relationship with God – pornography. Dave didn't like where this was going. He knew that he was one of those men. Although God had done a lot of transformation in his life, this was one sin that stubbornly clung to him, or maybe he stubbornly clung to it. The speaker urged the men to get serious about confessing and renouncing their addiction by also coming forward.

Now, it was one thing for Dave to clap and cheer for other guys, but it was entirely another to be the guy going forward, especially when it meant exposing a shameful secret.

"There's no way I'm going forward," Dave thought. "I'm a leader in my church. What would everyone think of me? I'd lose their respect." Dave continued to run down a list of reasons why he wasn't going to respond.

Then this thought went through his mind, "Are you more worried about what others think of you than what I think of you?" Dave started to move. Because of where he was sitting, he had to walk in front of a whole row of guys from his church and then past more rows as he headed down the aisle.

"What did I just do?" Dave thought. He took a quick look behind him expecting to see shocked faces. "What I saw, instead," Dave says, "was a line of guys from my church following me down the steps." Dave's act of integrity broke the dam and emboldened fifteen other men from his group to also step forward to confess their bondage to pornography and get clean.

Dave has learned that integrity can be difficult and painful at times. But every time he has been truthful, God has been faithful. God has strengthened Dave's character and his impact as a witness for Jesus who is "the Way the Truth and the Life."

## Make it Personal

- How would you define "integrity"? Who in your life would you say is a person of integrity? How are they a model for you?

- Have you ever been asked to "stretch the truth," or do something in your workplace that lacks integrity? How have you responded? How might God help you respond in the future?

- How does Proverbs 11:3 speak to these types of situations? In what ways can integrity guide you?

- In what area of your life might Jesus want you to be set free? Ask Him to reveal any hidden sin He wants you to surrender. As you're set free, ask Him to show you a trusted friend you can share this with to help you stay accountable.

- How has Jesus spoken to you in this devotional time?

## Prayer

Dear Jesus, you are the ultimate example of integrity. Please shape my character to be more like yours today. Help me to be a person of both grace and truth. Amen.

# KNOCK, KNOCK

## In the Word

Read Deuteronomy 4:29 and Matthew 7:7-8.

Jesus loves spiritual seekers. A seeker is a person who pursues God either out of sheer desperation or deep desire. They recognize that they have a void inside and they are looking for a true way to fill it.

Jesus loves seekers because He knows what will happen when they get serious about looking for the true God. When they seek Him, Jesus promises that they will find Him. He is not a God who likes to play Hide-and-Seek. He is a God who plays Seek-and-Find.

But Jesus waits until we're ready for Him. He doesn't break down the door of our heart demanding we let Him in. Instead He says, "I stand at the door and knock. If anyone hears my voice and opens the door, I will come in and eat with him, and he with me" (Revelation 3:20). Jesus waits until we're either desperate or desiring, or both.

If you are at the beginning of your spiritual quest, Jesus is knocking on the door of your heart, waiting for you to invite Him in. If you have been walking with Jesus for years, Jesus is waiting for you to let Him into areas of your life that you've kept closed off from Him. He wants to fill every area of your life with the joy and power of His presence. Do you hear that knock? Only you can answer the door.

## Judi Gavia's Story

As the first generation daughter of two Holocaust survivors, Judi was raised in a devout Orthodox Jewish home. They followed the laws of Torah closely, including keeping kosher, not spending money on the Sabbath and walking to synagogue instead of driving. Judi remembers her father, a rabbi, being so faithful to God. His love for God permeated everything he did.

But even as a young girl, Judi says, "I had many questions about the Jewish tradition and faith, which my father attempted to answer. But because of the unimaginable horrors he had endured in the Holocaust, I think it was hard for him to have me question anything about our faith."

Yet Judi continued to ask questions. Although she loved the way Judaism shaped her growing up years, Judi was still seeking something to fill the void she felt inside. As a teen and young adult, her search took her in many directions, including partying and pursuing a string of relationships. She also investigated a variety of spiritual paths, including EST, the Unitarian Church, and the New Thought Church (an eclectic spiritual organization). But still she felt empty.

Then came devastating news. In her mid-twenties, Judi was diagnosed with cervical cancer. "This really changed the trajectory of my life," she remembers. It caused her to seek out spiritual truth even more intently.

So Judi underwent surgery and cancer treatment, after which she received even more devastating news. Judi learned that as a result of the cancer, she could never have children. Judi was crushed. Even though she was not yet married, she still had hopes of one day having a family. Each time Judi watched another friend having a baby, "a little piece of me died inside," she says.

Eventually, Judi met and married Jerry, and they began their life together. A few years into their marriage, Judi began to have familiar pains. Thinking the cancer had returned, she went to see her doctor. Judi was amazed to learn that she did *not* have cancer. She was actually pregnant! "I recognized it as a miracle," Judi says, "but I didn't yet recognize from whom the miracle came." Judi continued seeking something to fill the void inside.

Shortly after their first son was born, Judi's mother unexpectedly passed away. At the same time, Judi also began experiencing serious difficulties in her marriage. As a new mother, dealing with the loss of her mom and struggling with relational problems, Judi needed help. "I had very few places I could go with my overwhelming grief and life challenges."

That's when Judi's neighbor, Betsy, began sharing with her about the love of Jesus Christ. Judi saw something in Betsy that intrigued her. Betsy had a peace and calmness about her in the storms of life. Judi wanted that peace and was desperate to find the source of it.

"So Betsy gave me the phone number of someone who worked at her church and encouraged me to call her," remembers Judi. In desperation, Judi overcame her normally reserved character and dialed the number. Rachel answered the phone, and Judi says she found herself "saying things about my life and situation that I had never shared with anyone else." After spending 45 minutes on the phone with a complete stranger, Judi found herself accepting an invitation to attend an investigative Bible study on the book of John.

"Shockingly, I said yes," Judi laughs. "But even more unbelievable to me is that I actually showed up for the study!" Attending a Bible study was somewhat intimidating for Judi, since she knew nothing about it and couldn't imagine being remotely like the other women who would be there. "I assumed they would all be theological wizards, and here I was the daughter of a rabbi."

What Judi discovered was that the women in the group were all at various stages of seeking as well. Some were new believers while others were still asking questions. Because the group was a safe place for Judi to ask questions, she kept showing up, week after week.

During that time, Judi was invited to attend a "Women of Faith" conference. Once again, she acted out of character and said yes. "From the moment I walked in the door, I started crying," she remembers. "And I'm not talking cute little tears. I'm talking big tears pouring down, gushing out the emptiness that I felt inside."

At the end of the conference, while everyone's eyes were closed in prayer, the speaker asked anyone who wanted a relationship with Jesus Christ and a changed life to raise their hand. "Before I knew it," Judi says, "my hand went up. And I can't even explain what happened, but I felt chills. I felt what I now know was the Holy Spirit, and I received the Lord."

Even though her new faith was an incredible gift, Judi began to struggle with turning her back on the faith of her parents, a faith that had brought them through the unspeakable horrors of the Holocaust. Then Judi met a couple who were also "completed Jews." "They helped me understand that just because I had Jesus as my Lord and Savior, it didn't mean that I had to turn my back on my heritage," Judi says. "Instead, it meant that it actually completed my heritage."

Judi has continued growing in her faith over the past fifteen years, and throughout that time she has learned that each time she studies God's word and incorporates her Jewish faith and tradition into her Christian faith, she is actually doing what Jesus did when He was on earth.

God honored Judi's honest search for the truth. As she looks back on her life, she can see how God lined things up in a way that led her to Jesus, the Messiah and Savior of the world. And she is grateful.

## Make it Personal

- In what ways can you relate to Judi's story? Where have you found yourself searching for God?

- What is motivating you more in your search for God – desperation or desire? How can God use these to draw you closer to Himself?

- What situations has God used in your life to get your attention? How have you responded to His knock on the door of your heart? Are there rooms in your heart that you still haven't allowed Him access to? What would it be like to open those doors today?

- How has Jesus spoken to you in this devotional time?

## Prayer

Dear Jesus, thank you that you are a God who loves to reveal yourself to us. Please give me a heart to seek you and find you today, and help me to allow you more fully into my life. Amen.

# PROTECTED

## In the Word

Read John 8:44 and Revelation 12:10 - *pay attention to how Satan's character is described ;* then read John 8:32 and Ephesians 6:14.

Satan loves a good lie, especially one that has a ring of truth to it. He will accuse and question and plant doubts in your mind.

- He will remind you of past sins, but remember, the truth is that they have been crucified with Christ. (Romans 6:6)
- He will tell you that you will fail, but remember, you can do all things through Christ who strengthens you. (Philippians 4:13)
- He will tell you that you're not loveable, but remember, you are so loved that Christ laid down his life for you. (John 10:15)
- He will tell you to give up because you can't win, but remember, greater is the One who is in you than the one who is in the world. (1 John 4:4)

For every lie Satan uses to try to knock you down, there is biblical truth that will set you free. You have already learned many of those truths over the past six weeks, and as you continue studying your Bible you will learn many more. Now, be sure to use those truths to armor yourself.

## John Orozco's Story

"Who do you think you are to be up here on stage? What makes you think you have any right to share with these people how to follow Christ? Remember all those times you blew it and failed to follow Him?"

John has heard these voices whispering in his ear. And each time he hears these lies, he runs back to the truth of God. "He reminds me of my call," says John. "And He tells me, 'you can believe those lies if you want, but that doesn't change your call. You've got a purpose.'"

Remembering this helps John to stand strong – not because He's so great or has it all together, but because God is so great and has given John everything he needs to do what God has called him to do.

So what is that call? If you had asked John that question eleven years ago, he would never have imagined the answer that is so clear to him today. God has called and gifted John to serve as the worship pastor at his church and as the leader of a Christian band called "Emissary" that travels and ministers to people while raising funds for an orphanage in Mexico.

Eleven years ago, when John was first asked to lead worship for his college group, he could only play three chords on the guitar. He hated it. In fact, each week he wanted to quit. But his girlfriend, now his wife, would encourage him and say, "You've got to go out there, you promised the pastor. You need to be a man of your word." So he kept going, and eventually began to love music. Today, he writes and arranges his own music and holds classes to teach others how to play guitar and keyboard.

But those voices still have a way of sneaking up on him, reminding him of things he's not proud of, ways he has failed God, himself, and others. And there's plenty to be reminded of. Before John decided to live for Christ, he wanted nothing to do with God. Even though he was raised by godly Christian parents, he went his own way in high school. He was more interested in partying with his friends and getting into drugs, alcohol and sex than getting to know Jesus.

But God was pursuing John, seeking to peel back the lies and let John know the truth of who God is and who God created John to be. More than once, people told John things like "God woke me up at 1:00 a.m. last night to pray for you." Often those prayers were prayed at the exact moments John needed it most.

He also remembers one night at a party, when the thought suddenly occurred to him that all the conversations around him were empty. In that moment, he could see that the things he was pursuing were all meaningless, passing away. He now knows those thoughts came directly from God.

So at the age of eighteen, John made the choice to be "all in" for Jesus. And since that day, it's been a journey to live into his calling and be the man God created him to be. He now has a clear sense of purpose, seeing that God can use him when he is willing to step out and trust.

But John would be the first to admit that just because he is a committed follower doesn't mean that he does it perfectly. There are moments when he's tempted to listen to the lies that he's not good enough and not worthy of telling others about Christ. He's seen how the enemy loves to exploit our weaknesses and keep us from living out our God-given purpose. The truth that helps John stay on course is the knowledge that God is still able to use him even though he has imperfections.

For example, John recognizes that he has a selfish streak, but he also sees how God is gradually changing that. "God has blessed me with children, and the whole process of raising kids is a process of self-denial. You learn that life is not about you," he says.

John is also encouraged by what happened on the night when Jesus was arrested. Jesus asked the disciples to wait and pray with him. "I believe the disciples wanted to follow Him and live in step with Him," says John. "And when they failed, Jesus said, 'the spirit is willing but the flesh is weak.' They were weak in that moment, but God was still able to use them. I finally came to the point where I realized that I'm weak, too. Even though I want to follow, I still fail. But I know that God's word is strong, and God is able to keep me strong. He can still use me, just like He used the disciples."

As John is willing to live into the truth of his calling, God continues to use him in powerful ways. One of the ministries John is most passionate about is a place called Gabriel House. It's a Mexican orphanage for about thirty kids with special needs. The couple who run the orphanage are doing the best they can to care for these kids, but they have very few resources.

He remembers his first trip there five years ago and how God touched his heart by a two-year-old girl named Lydia. She had nearly been strangled to death and had all kinds of physical challenges. "We got to hold her," John remembers, "and she was just shaking." John and his band mates found themselves in tears, their hearts broken by the needs of this little girl and all the children in that home. "My own daughter was almost the same age as Lydia," says John. "When I held Lydia, I felt like I was holding my own daughter. I wanted to provide for her as I would for my own daughter."

That trip began a journey for the Emissary band. Since that time, they have continued to hold concerts and sell CDs, with all the proceeds going to support Gabriel House. So far, they've been able to raise $30,000 over the past four years.

John returned to Gabriel House a few months ago and was amazed to see that Lydia was still there. The doctors had only given her two years to live. When John asked one of the workers about it, he was told that they believe the Lord has allowed Lydia to remain alive so that others like John would have their hearts broken for Gabriel House and God would use that to help provide for His precious little ones. "Even Lydia has purpose for her life," says John. "I want that, too – for every day to have purpose."

## Make it Personal

- The lies of the enemy can be powerful. What kinds of lies have you listened to in the past? How has this affected the way you see God? The way you see yourself? The way you see others?

- Given the types of lies you may have encountered, what are some of God's truths that can help you counter those lies? You may want to write these truths down and post them somewhere you'll see them often (like the bathroom mirror or the dashboard of your car).

- What can you learn from John's story that can help you in your journey with Jesus?

- How has Jesus spoken to you in this devotional time?

## Prayer

Dear Jesus, thank you for being the Truth. Help me to recognize any lies the enemy may be trying to deceive or accuse me with. Help me to turn away from those lies and keep my eyes fixed on you. Amen.

# ON the ROAD AGAIN

## In the Word

Read Psalm 16:11; Psalm 25:4-5; and Proverbs 3:5-6.

God's people have always been travelers.

And we can join the journey when we say yes to Jesus and "get on board" with Him. As we're traveling along the way, with *the* Way, we're stretched, encouraged and challenged. At some point, we also recognize that we don't have the ability to complete this journey on our own. That's when we begin to see that Jesus isn't just a traveling companion – He's our GPS, our directional guide, our North Star.

Whether you're traveling through a dark valley or enjoying the view on a mountaintop, Jesus is with you. He's saying, "Are you tired? Worn out?... Come to me. Get away with me and you'll recover your life... Keep company with me and you'll learn to live freely and lightly" (Matthew 11:28-30, *The Message*). Enjoy His company on your journey today, allow Him to fill you up and help you recover your life, and call on Him for directions – He knows the Way!

## Harmeet Barkschat's Story

In this week's "I Am" statement, Jesus says "I am the way..." But in *The Message* paraphrase that verse reads, "I am the *Road*..." Harmeet has been journeying with Christ for many years now, and part of her journey with God has involved some amazing times with Him in her car, out on the road. She has literally been on the road, traveling with "*the* Road" as her guide.

"I'm a 'Type A' personality," Harmeet admits. "I like to be in control. I like to be in the driver's seat. Often I would push God out of the way and get in the driver's seat myself. But I know that I need to let Jesus take the wheel."

One of those times when Jesus clearly took the wheel, happened back in 2001. Her daughter was sitting behind her, strapped into her car seat. As she approached a busy intersection, Harmeet had a green light, so she proceeded to go through the intersection. Suddenly an ambulance was coming straight at her from the cross street. Even though Harmeet did not have her radio on, for some reason she did not hear the siren until it was too late.

"My young daughter was sitting right behind me, and I realized that if they hit me, it would be on the side where we were both sitting," she says. "I could see fear in the eyes of the ambulance driver as he realized he was going to hit us."

At that moment, Harmeet experienced Jesus literally taking the wheel of her car. "Suddenly, we were parallel to the ambulance," she remembers. The only damage she ended up sustaining was a small crack in her front left turn signal. Harmeet was stunned.

"There was no way I could have moved the car like that," she says. "It could have been serious. I was shaking so badly, but I began praising the Lord because I knew there was no way I could have done that," she remembers, with tears of gratitude. "To Him, moving the car is such a little thing. But to us it could have been traumatic."

Just a few years earlier, in 1999, Harmeet began another adventure of faith – she started her own business. She is a cost accounting consultant, working with school districts. "My old business wanted me to stay," she says, "and they offered me a huge bonus. It was tough leaving a six-figure salary." But Harmeet sensed she was supposed to strike out on her own.

Then something unexpected happened. She began to get clients, but they were from farming country, several hours away. Even though Harmeet is originally from Fiji, she considers the San Francisco Bay area and Southern California to be more of her home turf. So to begin working in rural farming communities was a big change for her.

But once again, Jesus showed that he was in control of Harmeet's life. Now that she was working for herself, she had more freedom in how she conducted her business. "In my meetings with people, I have the freedom to talk to them about God," she says. "I could see why God wanted me there."

Not only is she able to talk about God on the job, but once again she finds her times in the car to be some of the most precious time of her day. "Some of the best prayer times I've had with God are when I'm alone in the car and I'm driving to far away clients, watching the sunrise and praising God."

But Harmeet doesn't stop at just praying with words. "Sometimes I'll raise my hand up in praise," she smiles and then quickly adds, "I still keep one hand on the wheel." Other times, Harmeet says, "I'll be crying – and of course I'll be thinking, 'oh no, I'm messing up my make up!' But I don't care. I'm just praising God."

This time alone with Jesus, "the Road," changes Harmeet's day. "When I walk into a school district office after time in my car," she says, "I'm so full of God because I've been praising Him on my drive. I know it makes a difference in how I relate to people. I'm so filled up."

Just recently, Harmeet's brothers had their own spiritual car experience. One of her brothers (who is not a Christian), has a transmission shop in Hawaii. Her other brother, a new believer, went to Hawaii to help with the shop. Each day as they drove the 45-minute commute to the shop, the brother who is a new believer read devotionals out loud from *Our Daily Bread*. Harmeet's other brother was a captive audience, listening to truth about God.

A few weeks ago, the brother who is not yet a believer contacted Harmeet and asked if she could get him some new *Our Daily Bread* devotionals since they had finished all the ones they owned. She was overjoyed that God is beginning to open his heart – and God began this good work, once again, in a car!

Whether she's on the road, out at work, or at home with her family, Harmeet's love for Jesus flows into all that she does. She sees that Jesus truly wants to be part of all of her life. "He's my shepherd, my provider," she says. "He takes care of me. It's like I'm a little sheep and he's going to provide for me and watch over me." What Harmeet most wants others to know about Jesus is that "He's not just your Lord and Savior – He can be your best friend, your confidant."

## Make it Personal

- Harmeet has journeyed with Jesus through highs and lows – what are some of the highs and lows God has seen you through? When are times, like Harmeet, that you are tempted to "take the wheel" of your life?

- In Psalm 25:4, what reason does the Psalmist give for wanting to know God's truth and His path? How is this reason true for you today?

- Read Proverbs 3:5-6. What are some ways you have leaned on your own understanding in the past? Where did this lead you? What might have been different if you had leaned on God's wisdom and direction instead?

- Where do you need God's guidance today? How can the passage from Proverbs help you find the guidance you need?

- How has Jesus spoken to you in this devotional time?

## Prayer

Dear Jesus, give me your peace and joy on the journey today. Help me to trust you more and let you be in the driver's seat. Amen.

a spiritual practice
# My Personal Compass

Jesus tells us that He is the Way, the Truth and the Life. As we follow Jesus, *the* way, it's also appropriate to seek God's way for us personally on this journey with Him. In different seasons of our lives, God's way may lead us in new directions, inviting us to let go of old ways so we can embrace new ones.

On our spiritual journey with Jesus, He seldom gives us a map to follow. Instead, He invites us to walk with Him and let Him guide us each step of the way. In this way, Jesus becomes our GPS or compass, helping us keep our bearings and make course corrections along the way.

## Getting Your Bearings

Today's spiritual practice involves time with God to regain your bearings. Take a piece of paper, as large as you'd like, and draw a large circle. Then, draw an X through the circle to divide it into four quadrants representing the four directions of a compass: north, south, east, and west. In the center, draw a small circle.

Feel free to keep this page simple or get more creative, using various colors of markers or pencils; you may also enjoy using magazine words or pictures, or other types of medium that help you express yourself.

Prayerfully considering the questions for each point on your compass. Then in each quadrant, write, draw, or collage about the thoughts, images, activities, people, events, choices, or questions that come to mind.

SOUTH: The direction of the sunny exposure, where you find your energy, imagination, spontaneity, and play. As you look this direction, ask yourself:

- Where is my creativity being called forth?
- What do I really long to do or be?
- How do I nurture myself? What are my passionate hobbies?
- Where do I find fun, play and rest? What makes me feel most alive?

NORTH: The North Star represents a guiding light, the stabilizing forces in your life. As you look this direction, ask yourself:

- Who is it that deeply loves and guides me?
- What are the images or pictures of God, or biblical scriptures that nurture and sustain me?
- Who are my spiritual guides and dearest friends?
- What is an important event in my faith journey and how has that given me guidance, direction, purpose or meaning?

WEST: The direction of the setting sun – this is the direction of endings and letting go. As you look this direction, ask yourself:

- What or who needs to be released, ended or shed in my life? (Maybe it's an old understanding or friendship that needs to go.)
- What beliefs, attitudes, habits and patterns do I need to die to?
- What maps no longer work for my life?
- Where is deep healing needed?

EAST: The direction of the rising sun – the direction of new beginnings. As you look this direction, ask yourself:

- What new energy or movement is starting to emerge in me?
- What new thing is starting to happen, and what am I taking hold of?
- Where am I being called to embrace something new?
- Am I aware of issues or areas in need of healing or change?

IN THE CENTER: As you "stand" in the center, prayerfully reflect on the following: In which direction do I feel attracted? Where is the energy for me on this compass? Where am I struggling? Where am I saying yes?

Ask God to help you let go of things that need to be released, and embrace the things He is calling you to. If you're able, write the word "YES" in the center of the circle to represent your desire before God.

# "I Am the True Vine"

His face was deeply lined from the years he had spent in the sun. His posture was a bit hunched, but he was still strong. His eyes squinted as he walked down the rows and carefully, lovingly inspected each vine in his vineyard.

He smiled as he held some of the fruit in his grizzled hand. The large, deep purple of the grapes stood out in sharp relief against his dark olive skin. They were just about ripe. He was certain that the juice they'd produce would make the best wine in the kingdom.

These plump, beautiful grapes didn't happen by accident. They were the result of years of careful attention by his hands. He was a master vinedresser. He had learned his craft from his father and had perfected it over decades. Each vine in his vineyard had been carefully shaped day after day, year after year to produce the abundant crop he was proudly inspecting.

He remembered when he first planted this vine so many years ago and how he had carefully tied the branches up so they would get the maximum amount of sunlight to grow and thicken. As he looked at one of the branches sagging under the weight of the thick bunches of grapes, he remembered how it had come loose and fallen down into the mud. If the branch had been allowed to remain there it would have become sickly and never produced fruit. But he had found the branch and gently lifted it so he could wash off the dirt. Then he tied it back up where it could once again thrive as it soaked in the life-giving sun.

He thought about the early harvests from this vine. Although it was good to see the vine starting to produce, he knew that with proper care there were even better years ahead. While the early fruit was good, the fruit he now held in his hand was exceptional and abundant, at least four times what the vine used to produce.

As he looked at the shape of the vine, he remembered each snip and cut he had made. If he hadn't pruned away all those extraneous shoots, this vine would be all leaves and no fruit. It would look good, but worth nothing. All the extra branches and leaves would have diverted away the life-giving sap from the fruit, so if it had fruit at all, it would have been tiny and sour. But since he was a master vinedresser, he knew exactly where and when to prune the branches so that they would produce rows of rich, dark, juicy grapes.

The vinedresser straightened up. As his eyes gazed over his vines bursting with fruit, he let out a long breath of satisfaction. This is what he had worked for. This is what he had looked forward to. This was the purpose of the vine and the goal of the vinedresser. He swelled with pride and let out a laugh of joy as he savored the results.

Jesus said, "I am the true vine and my Father is the vinedresser. It is to my Father's glory that you bear much fruit." That is the purpose of the vine and the goal of the vinedresser.

# SIGNIFICANCE

## In the Word

Read John 15:1-11.

We were made to be significant. In Jesus' metaphor of the vine, we are meant to be fruitful. An unfruitful branch is a waste of a branch, and an insignificant life is a waste of a life. Being significant can put a lot of stress and pressure on a person as they strive to make something of themselves. But the metaphor of the vine isn't a picture of striving, but remaining.

It is the presence of Jesus in your life that makes you significant. Think about it, why is the White House famous? It's not because it's white. It's famous because the President of the United States lives there. In the same way, it's the presence of Jesus that makes us significant. And it is Jesus' presence that allows us to do significant things.

As you nourish your relationship with Jesus, you'll naturally serve Him out of love. And through loving service, you will make a significant difference in the lives others, even as Jesus is making a difference in your life.

## William Ingersoll's Story

The old saying, "you can't keep a good man down" certainly applies to William. Even though he is retired, he hasn't slowed down at all. He is a leader at his church, has led the singing for the congregation, and leads a weekly small group Bible Study. Outside church, William is the President of the local Toastmasters Club.

William also has a sixth sense for people who are hurting, and rather than shying away from them, he comes alongside them, ready to listen to their struggles and offer support and encouragement. In William's back pocket you will always find a copy of the Gospel of John. He is ready at a moment's notice to pull it out and give it away while sharing with people the difference Jesus has made in his life, and can make in theirs as well.

None of this would be that amazing until you discover that William is an introvert at heart, a fact that shocks most people who didn't know William "back then."

William grew up in the Roman Catholic Church where he served as an altar boy for ten years and developed a strong faith in Jesus. He credits his Catholic upbringing for teaching him to appreciate and revere the majesty and glory of Jesus. But it wasn't until he was in high school and started attending a Christian club called Young Life that he started learning about having a personal relationship with this majestic and mighty Jesus.

After high school, William stopped attending his Catholic church, not because he was walking away from God. He wanted to discover more about developing a personal relationship with Jesus and he didn't feel the Catholic Church could help him.

William dabbled in churches, visiting here and there, but never settling anywhere. It was years later that he and his wife, Debbie, were invited by friends to visit their church. That was in 1979 and William and Debbie have been going to that church ever since.

William was extremely introverted. You might even call him a "stealth Christian." For William, attending church meant popping in on Sunday morning after church started and people were singing, sitting in the back row, and then immediately popping out when the service was over, barely noticed. However, his wife was, in William's words, "gregarious and needed more people contact."

Finally, after several years, William relented and agreed to go to a small group Bible study that met in someone's home. William smiles as he says, "I told the group that I was only there because my wife needed to be around more people."

For months, William sat in that Bible study, listening, occasionally nodding his head, but barely saying a word. But the warmth and friendliness of the group began to wear him down. He started to venture a comment or two, until he became a fully participating member of the group.

The group relit William's passion to develop a deeper, more personal relationship with Jesus. He could tell that others in the group had that kind of relationship. He could hear it in their words and see it in their behavior. William had always believed in Jesus, but now he was falling in love with Jesus. "I was amazed that the mighty God of the universe *wanted* to have a deep and personal relationship with me," William says.

As an introvert, William was always worried about how others might perceive him. He was afraid of being noticed. But his small group Bible study experience encouraged him to believe that people may actually perceive him in positive ways. As William grew in his awareness of Jesus' presence in his life, he began to want to worship Him with less caution and reserve. It was then he made a big, faith-stretching move (at least for an extreme introvert).

William moved from the back row of the church to the front row, and then started to sing with gusto. This led to singing in the choir, which led to leading the congregation in singing, which led to even more faith-stretching opportunities.

As William became more aware of the real presence of Jesus in his life, Jesus transformed his introversion from a weakness to a strength. William can now speak in front of groups, but what he enjoys the most is individual relationships where he can counsel, support, encourage and love people one -on-one.

William's motto is, "Vocatus atque non vocatus Deus aderit," which is Latin for "Bidden or unbidden, God is present." It is that realization that has transformed his life from being a "stealth Christian" to being someone who is making a difference.

When asked what difference Jesus' presence has made in his life, William says, "Everything. I draw my hope and joy from knowing that Jesus is in me, rather than from the circumstances around me. I have confidence because I know Jesus is present. And I have peace because I know that I can trust my life, my family, my needs, and my circumstances to Jesus."

Today, William is retired, but he hasn't slowed down. Ever since connecting to Jesus and Jesus' family after joining that Bible study years ago, William has been energized by Jesus' presence in his life. Every time he gets an opportunity to be used by God to bless someone else, it fires him up. He knows that "Bidden or unbidden, God is present." And because he has experienced the difference Jesus' presence makes, he makes it his mission to help others discover that presence as well.

There was a time that William was so trapped inside his introversion that he was insignificant. But as he grew in his awareness of Jesus' presence , he was transformed and became a leader, able to bear fruit and make a difference in the lives of others. Jesus can do the same for you.

## Make it Personal

- In today's story, what kinds of fruit do you notice in William's life? How did his relationship with Christ allow him to experience so much fruit?

- In the metaphor of the vine and the branches, Jesus reveals that fruit does not come from our striving, but from the life He pours into us. Where in your life are you striving these days? In what ways might Jesus be inviting you to surrender some of your striving and strife-filled activities?

- In what areas of your life are you seeing fruit? How is Jesus involved in that? How can you allow Him to be even more involved?

- How has Jesus spoken to you in this devotional time?

## Prayer

Dear Jesus, thank you for being the Vine, and for offering me all the life and energy I need to do the things you call me to do. Please help me remain connected to you and allow you to produce your fruit in my life. Amen.

# STAY CONNECTED

## In the Word

Read John 15:1-6 and Mark 12:28-34.

We are called to love God by giving Him our all – our whole heart. But when your life is going well, and there are no crises driving you to God, it's easy to start going through the motions in your relationship with Him. First your prayer life starts to slip, then reading your Bible is forgotten. Church becomes less important. After all, you don't want it dominating your life. You need balance, right?

Jesus offers a caution. If you start to lose your connection to Him, drastic measures will become necessary, not as a punishment, but to restore you to fruitfulness. How drastic of a measure will depend on how much it takes to get your attention. It could be anything from a mild pruning, to cutting and burning.

But if you return to the Vine, if you seek God with ALL your heart, soul, mind and strength, God will restore you to fruitfulness. But better still is to always remain a fully devoted follower of Jesus and become someone who experiences "much fruit."

## Brian Pedersen's Story

It was Brian's first Father's Day since his quadruplets were born, but Brian wasn't home to see them. He was in a 30-day alcohol rehabilitation program. Brian comes from a family of alcoholics. His mom and dad are both alcoholics and his brother died of alcoholism.

Given that kind of history, Brian knew better, but he started drinking anyway and couldn't stop. He'd get on binges and disappear from his family for days. Finally, he admitted he had a problem and went to rehab, but it was too little, too late to save his marriage.

After rehab, Brian started doing everything right. He joined AA and even went to church. But he never took his relationship with Jesus seriously. Brian was a "rabbit hole Christian." He would pop in on Sunday mornings, listen to the message, and then pop back out. "What else was needed?" he thought.

As Brian got sober, things got better for him. His job was good, money was good, kids were good, and everything seemed to be going well. But after he'd been sober for four years, he started to coast. He would skip church because he "didn't want to miss the football game." He'd skip AA meetings because "he had to work." He even started having a glass of wine at dinner because he could "handle it now."

One glass of wine became two, then four, then a bottle and he was hooked again. Maybe you've heard the old joke, "I can stop whenever I want. I've already done it a hundred times." That described Brian. He would quit for awhile, only to go on a binge that lasted days at a time. Until he went on a binge that lasted eleven-days.

He landed in a hospital emergency room near death. As he lay on a gurney with IV's attached to both arms, he thought, "My mom is going to have to go to the funeral of another son who died of alcohol."

It was at that moment that Brian had a spiritual awakening. He sensed Jesus telling him, "You can keep drinking and die, or you can choose to quit and follow me." In that moment, Brian chose to follow Jesus.

After surviving this scare, Brian went back to AA and church, but this time things were different. Before, Brian had just gone through the motions at church. He never sought a personal relationship with Jesus. He never spent time in prayer, or read the Bible, or sought to connect with others who could teach him more about a life with Jesus. As a result, Jesus wasn't real to Brian. Brian knew a little *about* Jesus, but he didn't actually *know* Jesus.

Today, Brian no longer goes through the motions. He is actively pursuing a relationship with Jesus and seeking to do God's will.

Brian doesn't go to bed at night without saying prayers of thanks, and in the morning he doesn't start his day without reading the Bible and getting on his knees to pray. He thanks God for giving him the chance to live, to be a father and a friend. He asks God for the wisdom and strength to make right choices.

"In the past," Brian says, "I used to only pray '911 prayers' when I was drunk and in desperate need. Now, I'm praying all day long."

As Brian grows in his relationship with Jesus, he can see the difference it is making in his life. He has an inner strength he's never known before. In his previous years of sobriety, he had constantly struggled to resist the temptation to drink, a struggle he eventually lost. Now, the temptations are fewer and they don't have the enticing power they once had. Brian is delighted to find out that he's able to dismiss the temptations rather than ruminate on them and allow them to take root.

What's made the difference between the last time he was sober and this time? As far as Brian is concerned, it's the time he's spending in prayer, Bible study, serving and going to church. Through these activities, he is building his relationship with Jesus, the true Vine. He's no longer just going through the motions and doing his duty. Now it's real. And Brian is ready to take his next step of growth. He just joined a men's Bible study group, and he's bringing a couple of friends with him.

## Make it Personal

- Just like Brian, we each have activities, behaviors, addictions, habits, or thought patterns that can pull us away from seeking Christ. What kinds of things seek to pull you away? How can you stay more connected to Christ so these negative things lose their pull on you?

- When Brian slowly stopped going to church and seeking God, he found ways to rationalize his actions. When have you done the same thing? What are your prized excuses and rationalizations for this type of behavior?

- Read Mark 12:29-34. What does Jesus say are the most important commandments? What would it look like in your life if you were to actively pursue living these out?

- How has Jesus spoken to you in this devotional time?

## Prayer

Dear Jesus, I know that I don't have the power to change myself. I need your to help. Please show me how to love you more, and how to receive your love for me. Keep me close to you today. Amen.

# JOYFULLY HUMBLED

## In the Word

Read John 15:9-13; Philippians 2:5-8.

When a grapevine is healthy and well-tended, it produces fruit. When there is no fruit, something is wrong.

The same is true in our lives. If we are connected to the Vine, Christ will naturally produce His fruit in our lives. When there's no fruit, something is wrong.

This means that when we are in Christ, we become really fruity! But the key is staying connected to the Vine. We don't grow fruit by trying harder, we grow fruit by abiding in Christ. And Galatians 5:22 gives us a small taste of the delicious fruit we can expect to see. It says, "The fruit of the Spirit is love, joy, peace, patience, kindness, goodness, faithfulness, gentleness, and self-control."

That's quite a list – and it's just the beginning of all that God wants to do in our lives.

## Joy Champion's Story

God is teaching Joy to feel what others feel and to reach out in love as she walks with God through some difficult life circumstances.

Although in the past she has suffered the pain of infertility and breast cancer, at times it's felt more painful for Joy to experience relational challenges, such as those times when she felt misunderstood or treated unjustly. But Joy is discovering that "when I die to self, I'm dying to my desires and ego, and I'm able to live for Christ's desires."

As Christ is changing Joy, her response to misunderstanding is different than it once was. "Now when I'm misunderstood, I have a security in Christ," she says, "and I know that God knows my heart; He knows that my intentions are good. I don't have to worry what others think."

One of the ways Christ is helping Joy to find her security and identity in Him is by teaching Joy about humility. "Humility is what draws people to Christ," she observes. "This doesn't mean we should let people walk all over us, it means to speak the truth in love, but also accept people where they are. To love them and pray for them – and not think that I am God."

This type of attitude does not come naturally to Joy. "For many years, I was following Christ and His word," she says, "but it was all head knowledge. I had become self-righteous and judgmental." Now Joy is learning to get up every morning and surrender her day to God, knowing that He wants to use her to draw people to Himself.

But Joy quickly admits that she is still in the process of being changed by Christ. "If I'm arrogant or if I come across that way – and that can still happen, because I haven't arrived – I can always go back," she says. "In humility I can go back and apologize and ask for forgiveness and reach out in love."

In addition to humility, God has been teaching Joy about humiliation. She describes humiliation as the experience of "being unjustly treated or disrespected." Joy sees Jesus as a good example. "Humiliation is being stripped of your worth by others or in front of others. That's when you really have to find your security in the Lord. I know that God loves me, and so He has allowed me to be humiliated at times so that He could accomplish His good work in my life."

The experience of humiliation is something Joy believes everyone will experience at some point in life, especially as we get older. "I think old age is a way God uses to teach us humiliation," she observes. Joy saw this truth lived out as she watched her dad grow older. He was a decorated World War II fighter pilot and a distinguished Southern gentleman, but as he got older he could no longer get around on his own. Joy would have to take him places. "He would go in his wheelchair and have his oxygen on his lap and he'd pick up his hearing aid," Joy remembers. It was hard for her to watch her strong father deteriorate as he aged, and to know how humbling – and humiliating – it must be for him.

As hard as it can be, Joy is still grateful for the ways God uses humility and humiliation to work in and through her. More recently, she has been experiencing this anew in regard to cancer. After being cancer-free for sixteen years, Joy's cancer returned and metastasized to her liver. The doctors gave her six months to live – that was three years ago. Earlier this year, they discovered the cancer had spread to her brain, so they put a port in her chest through which she could receive chemo treatments.

One day as she was teaching a class at church, her face began to grow quite large. When she looked at herself in the mirror, she remembers thinking, "I guess this is how I'm going to look now." That humble reaction to her shocking appearance was something she would not have had years ago.

When she went in for her next chemo appointment, the nurses couldn't insert the needle into her port. Then suddenly, Joy passed out on the floor. They rushed her by ambulance to the hospital, thinking something was wrong with her brain. But after running a CT scan, they discovered a blood clot had formed around her port, causing blood to flow to her brain with no way to come back down.

"That's why my head was so big," she laughs. Joy can see so many ways God has been working in her life through her journey with cancer. She's also grateful that "He is protecting me from having a big head – in more ways than one!"

As Joy continues to surrender her life to God and find her identity in Christ, she experiences a deep security and peace, which leads her to make a remarkable statement: "I'm not afraid to die," she says boldly. "Not one bit afraid. I think that takes total security. At the end of my life and I go to be with God, standing at the throne – well, I'm really looking forward to that," she says. "It's helping me to give up this world, to see how insignificant the things of this world are. That's a journey God teaches you."

As a result of Joy's openness to God's work in her life, He has been able to use her to encourage many others. Currently she serves as the Pastor of congregational care at her church, and recently God allowed her to minister to a woman in a nursing home who had become angry and bitter and was afraid to die. "I don't even remember what I said," Joy recalls, "but God used me to set her free from her fear."

When Joy reflects on her life, she says, "I think God has allowed me to go through the things I have, because it's a way that He draws people to Himself through me." Joy's love for God and heart for His people shine clearly through her words and actions, and the fruit of Joy's life continues to grow.

## Make it Personal

- One kind of fruit that Christ is producing in Joy is humility. As others observe your life these days, what types of fruit might they see?

- Jesus Christ is not only our Vine, but He's also our model for how to live life. In Philippians 2:5-8, what attitudes and behaviors does Christ display? From today's story, how do you see Joy following Christ's example? How can you follow His example?

- According to John 15:9-13, how can you experience the joy of Christ?

- How has Jesus spoken to you in this devotional time?

## Prayer

Dear Jesus, please help me to remain in you today so that you can produce your good fruit in my life. Keep me humble before you, recognizing that I can do nothing apart from you. Amen.

# ABIDING in CHRIST

## In the Word

Read John 15:4-5; Mark 1:35; I Thessalonians 5:16-18.

When Jesus invites us to abide in Him, He explains the reason for it by saying, "apart from me you can do nothing."

That may seem like an overstatement, until we remember that Jesus Himself spent time abiding with His Father, often slipping away to spend time alone with Him. If Jesus needed to stay connected, how much more do we need to do so?

As Margaret Feinberg says in *Scouting the Divine:* "The vine is the source of everything for the branch – every nutrient, every life-giving drop of water, every hint of growth. The branch is completely dependent on the vine. But even in those moments when I grow wild or unbalanced, God is faithful as a vinedresser to perform all the small cuts I need to remain faithful. So in that place where I am abiding in Christ under the watchful eye of the Father, I can trust that the Father will be pruning those areas and desires in my life that don't line up with where he wants me to go."

## Cathy Squire's Story

Cathy has never been one to take her faith lightly. Even though she grew up in a strong Christian home in Hong Kong, she wasn't content to simply accept the faith of her parents. She had to find out for herself if it was all true. So beginning at the age of fifteen, she began asking lots of questions.

Her parents weren't worried, though, because they knew if she searched long enough, she would discover the truth for herself.

Years later, while studying at UC Berkeley, Cathy attended a Chinese for Christ conference, and during that event, "what the speaker was talking about made sense to me," she remembers. "It was like I had half of a page of writing and the other half had been torn off – but suddenly the Christian faith gave me the half I was missing so that now the page made sense."

From that time on, Cathy began to grow in her faith by learning to stay in communion with Christ throughout the day. "Maybe it sounds simplistic," she says, "but that verse in I Thessalonians 5:17 that says we should 'pray without ceasing' was my first introduction to prayer."

She began to learn what it means to abide in Christ by keeping Jesus in her mind and heart throughout the day, allowing Him to speak to her through every day experiences, the ordinary stuff of life. "All of life belongs to God," she explains, "so when my awareness is open to God, He can speak to me through many different things."

A great example of this happened for Cathy just recently. She and her husband had a "volunteer" squash plant spring up in their backyard this past summer. They were not able to tend the plant as carefully as they might normally have done, but this plant proved that it didn't need much tending. It ended up producing more than 250 squash over the summer.

Cathy reflected on this plant and the abundant crop and how it might relate in some way to her life. She asked God, "What do you want to speak to me about through this abundant squash?" She kept these thoughts to herself, but also kept her heart open to hear from God. As she was pondering this, her husband, Bill, said, "Wow, look at that squash! It's like God saying, 'My abundant love is upon your life.'" Cathy was filled with joy, because she knew God was speaking to her through Bill, confirming things she sensed God say about His abundant love for her.

Cathy has learned that anytime she is open to noticing things, God can speak to her. "Everything that comes to us through our five senses, and the things we think and feel all have bearing on our life together with God," she explains.

In addition to paying attention to God throughout her day, Cathy has learned to abide in Christ through a number of spiritual practices that keep her heart open to Him. Cathy is quick to share though, that she's not always as disciplined as she would like to be in these spiritual practices. But the more she pursues them, the more connected she feels to Christ, and the more of God's fruit she sees in her life.

One of the spiritual practices that has helped Cathy keep growing in her faith is reading scripture. For many years she has read one chapter of Proverbs, one Psalm, another passage from the Old Testament, and a passage from the New Testament each day. In this way, she works her way regularly through the entire Bible, allowing God to speak to her through a variety of biblical texts. There have also been times when Cathy has found it helpful to read through a daily devotional, such as *My Utmost For His Highest*, as a way to listen for God speaking.

Throughout the years, Cathy has expanded her spiritual practices to include such things as the Prayer of Examen and Lectio Divina (each described in this book on Day 21 and Day 28). These types of prayers are known as "contemplative prayers," since they are focused on listening for God's voice.

More recently, Cathy is finding that God is giving her a special gift for intercessory prayer, which focuses more on praying for the needs of others. "In the course of the day, different people come into my heart and I sense this affection and love for them, and then a prayer will rise up in me. I have a strong desire to pray for them," she shares. "This has been such a delight to me, and I'm very thankful to God."

Cathy has been walking with Christ since 1967, and throughout the years one of the most amazing blessings she has experienced has been a continual sense of His presence with her. This constant companionship brings her great peace and joy, and helps her to abide in Him.

At times, abiding in Christ has meant experiencing the pain of being on the cross with Christ. Other times, it has meant being in the tomb with him, in a time of waiting. "And of course, I love the rising with Him," she smiles. "I don't think I could have walked through some of the challenging things I have without Christ's presence with me."

One of those challenging times for Cathy came when she was working on accumulating her counseling hours in order to take the Marriage and

Family Therapy licensing exam. When she totaled her hours, she had more than the required 3,000 hours – but then she discovered she was three months past the deadline for acquiring them. She was deeply discouraged.

At that time, God gave her the image of a gardener looking over a grapevine, and instead of pruning branches, he was pruning some of the fruit so that other fruit could be more plump and juicy. "Even though there is disappointment in letting some things go," she says, "I sensed God telling me that He was taking away some of the fruit so that the life of the plant could go to the other fruit."

Once again, Cathy was grateful for God's assurance that He was with her, watching over her and abundantly providing for her. This helped her let go of her desire to be a Marriage and Family Therapist and remain open to other ministries and opportunities God has brought through the years. And the fruit continues to grow.

## Make it Personal

- What parts of Cathy's story intrigue you or give you ideas on how to stay connected?

- I Thessalonians 5:17 tells us we should pray without ceasing. How is this possible? What might that look like in your life?

- What do you learn about the importance of prayer from Mark 1:35? How is Jesus a model for us of abiding?

- If you're able, go for a walk and notice any plants that you see. What do you notice about healthy, thriving plants? Dying plants? Pruned plants? What might God be saying to you through these living lessons? Which plant seems to represent you today?

- How has Jesus spoken to you in this devotional time?

## Prayer

Dear Jesus, thank you that you supply all the strength, love, peace, joy, and life that I need. Please help me to abide in you today and stay open to listening for what you may want to say to me. Amen.

# A NEW CEO

## In the Word

Read John 15:1-3, 9-14; I John 2:3-6.

Jesus did not leave us in the dark about how we can remain in Him. We remain in Christ through obedience, but not forced obedience. Authentic obedience will be motivated by our love for Jesus and His love for us.

It's a simple recipe. When we obey we remain, when we remain we are fruitful, and when we are fruitful we are joyful.

Too often, we seem to treat obedience to Christ as a burden or enslavement. Jesus wants us to see that it is just the opposite. Obedience, motivated by love, leads to blessing.

## Steve Lindner's Story (Part 2)

Steve was a business owner who cared about one thing – himself. He would do whatever was needed to obtain more income and pleasure for himself even if it was unethical or, in some cases, illegal. If it meant lying, he would lie. If it meant cheating, he would cheat.

To avoid paying worker's compensation, he treated his employees as sub-contractors. That way, if one of his employees was hurt on the job, they were on their own. He really didn't care what happened to them unless it was going to cost him something or get him something. Was that unethical? Certainly. Was it illegal? Possibly. But his business was about one thing – himself.

In Steve's line of business, there were many government standards to uphold. But being in compliance with all of those standards would have damaged his profits. So Steve did the minimum necessary to make it *look* like he was in compliance, knowing all along that he was nowhere close to meeting government standards and that he was putting his workers and customers at risk. He reasoned that he was only doing what was necessary to stay in business.

Despite his large profits, Steve was always feeling stress. He lived and died over each account that came in or left. No matter how much he made, it wasn't enough. Since he wasn't happy, he figured that he simply needed more money. He put his heart and soul into his business and ignored his family. This left his family in shambles, creating yet more stress in his life.

Adding even more to the stress were all the lies and deceit he had to manage and worry about. If he got caught, the fines and loss of business would ruin him. So he lived in constant fear of being discovered.

As the stress continued to build, Steve finally realized how badly he needed Jesus in his life and he prayed to commit his life to following Christ. That single decision began to change everything for Steve, including his work.

Steve quickly realized he needed to completely restructure the way he did business. It was a radical transformation. He started by filing new incorporation papers with the state that listed himself as president but Jesus Christ as CEO. Steve wanted to officially put in writing who was really in charge of his business. By doing that, Steve says, "It's held me to a higher standard."

The changes Steve made to run his business in a God-honoring way were costly. But the cost didn't matter anymore. (That statement in itself shows how much Steve was changing). Steve was now serving Jesus. The changes had to be done.

One of the costs involved dealing with his workers fairly. He moved them from being sub-contractors to employees. As a result, his workmen's comp expenses went from $500 to $9,000 a month.

"I didn't have an extra $9,000 a month lying around," Steve said. "I really wasn't sure how I was going to make it work. I just knew it was the right thing to do." Steve reasoned that it was God's business now. Steve's job was to make sure he was being a good steward of the business, but the results were up to God.

Within months Steve had figured out ways to streamline the business that had never occurred to him before. On top of that, new business started coming in. Between the cost savings and new business, Steve more than made up for the expense of coming into compliance.

Steve said, "I didn't make those changes in order to get God to bless me. I made them because I realized I had been wrong and wanted to change in order to honor God." Steve didn't demand anything from God in return for the sacrifices he was making. In fact, he expected the changes to really cost him and believed that he deserved to have them cost him. So, when the blessings of new business and profit unexpectedly came along, Steve was surprised and grateful.

By putting his business in the hands of his CEO, Jesus Christ, Steve discovered the difference Jesus made. As a result, Steve has learned to trust Jesus with his business and his life. One example of trusting the business to Jesus came when his salesperson left the company. Steve had a strong sense that he wasn't supposed to hire a new one, even though not having a salesperson gathering new business seemed crazy to Steve. Yet Steve was learning to follow God's lead, and this seemed like a strong direction from God. To Steve's surprise, business actually went up even though he no longer had a salesperson.

To this day, Steve doesn't have a sales force. He feels he is supposed to leave that part of the business in God's hands as an act of faith. He's quick to add that he doesn't believe this is what all Christian business owners should do to show their faith. This is a unique walk of faith between Steve and God.

Maybe the greatest blessing Steve has experienced since he began honoring God with His business practices is that his stress is gone. Steve no longer looks over his shoulder, afraid that he's about to get caught. And he no longer lives and dies with every little up or downtick of his business. He's learned to do his best and leave the results to God.

Steve's business used to be all about him, yet he never achieved the happiness he desired. Now, Jesus is the CEO of his business, and that has made all the difference. Business is good and Steve's life is great. In fact, he has a hard time imagining that it could possibly get better.

## Make it Personal

- From I John 2:3-6, how do we know if we have truly come to know Christ?

- What do you learn about obedience from Steve's story? What is the fruit of his obedience?

- In John 15:9-11, what is the fruit we receive when we are obedient?

- In what areas of your life right now are you able to be obedient to Christ? How does this affect your relationship with Him?

- In what areas of your life do you sense God revealing your need for more obedience? What will you do about that?

- How has Jesus spoken to you in this devotional time?

## Prayer

Dear Jesus, thank you for the joy you offer when I remain in you and follow your ways. I want more of your joy in my life. Please help me to be more obedient to you today and allow you to have your way in my life. Amen.

# JOY-FULL

## In the Word

Read John 15:9-11.

Who doesn't want to experience joy? It is one of our deepest desires. Yet joy can be so elusive.

Joy is what you experience when your deepest needs are met and you experience unconditional love. When you experience fulfillment, direction, security, a second chance, and a sense of purpose, you will feel joy. This is why Jesus said, "If you want to experience joy, remain in me."

When you remain in Jesus, His presence will meet your deepest needs and you will experience a joy that comes from inside, a joy that is not held hostage to circumstances. You cannot hide a joy like that. It will be seen on your face, heard in your voice, and felt in your serving. It is what Jesus calls "complete joy."

## John Burke's Story (with his daughter, Haley)

John has a big smile on his face as he looks around at the sight of families having fun together. John is the Director of Camp Challenge, a camping experience for adult cancer patients and their families. It's a chance for them to enjoy a weekend away from all the stress that comes with having cancer, while having fun and making family memories. For one weekend they can put aside the "what ifs" and the "how longs" and even the "How will I pay for this?" (Camp Challenge is free). Instead, they simply get to enjoy having fun together as a family.

Watching the smiles appear on people's faces as the dark clouds lift from their lives for at least a weekend is a joy John finds almost indescribable. Even better is having his family there to serve alongside him. He watches with satisfaction as his wife chats with the wife of a cancer patient and his daughters laugh and play with their kids. These are precious memories.

Being Director of Camp Challenge is not just a job to John, it is a passion. He doesn't even get paid, he's a volunteer. But he is thrilled to have this opportunity to use his God-given gifts in such a meaningful way.

According to author Frederick Buechner, we can recognize God's calling in our lives as, "the place where your deep gladness and the world's deep hunger meet." This describes what John has found. Through Camp Challenge, and the Me-One Foundation that sponsors it, John has found the "deep gladness" of God's calling in his life. He's in his sweet spot.

Yet there was nothing sweet about the road that led John here. Just a few years ago, John himself was a camper at Camp Challenge.

John remembers the day he walked into his doctor's office to receive some test results. The look on his doctor's face tipped him off that it wasn't going to be good news. But he still wasn't prepared for how bad the news was. The doctor explained to him that he had pancreatic cancer and that he needed to go home and set his affairs in order because he had six months – at most – to live.

It was devastating news. He was still young and his daughters were only four and eight years old. But John and his wife, Jen, had a rock-solid faith in Jesus – a faith that would give them strength even as it was being tested. They began praying, not only for healing, but also for wisdom and guidance, and they surrounded themselves with the support of their friends and church.

John especially recalls the strength he received from the men in his small group Bible study. John says, "If I needed to call someone in the middle of the night just to talk or even to cry, they always answered the phone and never complained."

Jesus was their rock. As the days went by, John and Jen leaned more and more on God, praying for the best and preparing for the worst. "Not our will, but yours be done," they prayed.

An answer to the prayer came when John was directed to a surgeon who was performing a new surgery that could save his life. But it was a radical procedure and there was a real chance that John would not survive the operation. Still, they chose to take the chance. John still remembers the pain of sitting on the couch with his daughters the night before the surgery, realizing that this could be goodbye. That was six years ago.

It was during his recovery from surgery that John heard about Camp Challenge. For the next two years, he and his family went as campers and experienced the blessed relief and encouragement that the Camp Challenge weekend provided. John remembers that it was at camp that he saw his daughters smile for the first time since hearing about the cancer. That moment was priceless. After two years as a camper, John decided it was time to give back, so he started volunteering to serve each year at the camp. Now, he is the Camp Director.

"Without the presence of Jesus, and the support of my church, I don't know how I would have made it through that time," John says. And that's the message he gets to share with the campers each year at Camp Challenge. Although it is not a Christian camp, as Camp Director John is able to tell his own cancer story and share about the difference Jesus has made in helping him deal with it all.

Because of his experience, John knows better than most that every new day of life is a gift. His cancer is not gone – it could reappear at any time. But rather than letting anxiety eat away at him, he has learned to trust his life to Jesus' safekeeping.

Because John recognizes that his life is a gift, he tries to make the most of what he's been given. The result of that approach has actually made the past few years of his life the most rewarding. He can't imagine his marriage being stronger, and as far as sisters go, his daughters are incredibly close.

John's younger daughter, Haley, now ten years old, remembers when they first began this journey together as a family. "My dad told people that God was going to make everything okay," she shares. John's faith helped a very young Haley develop her faith. Haley goes on to say that "God is now my life. I can talk to Him just as easily as I talk to anyone else." This is a true gift that many adults long for.

Haley and her sister Ashley have also learned from their dad that it's important to pass the blessings along. So now, Haley says, "it makes me feel really good to help other kids and their parents at camp. I can understand what they are going through." At ten years old, Haley is learning to let God use her to make a difference.

John smiles as he thinks about all that has happened. Although it's been a difficult road, John has stayed faithful to Jesus, and he has seen Jesus be faithful to him. Now, he gets to enjoy his "sweet spot" for yet another day.

## Make it Personal

- What deep needs did Jesus meet in John's life that has allowed him to be so joyful?

- What deep needs has Jesus met in your life that have helped you be joyful? What needs has Jesus met these past fifty days as you have grown closer to the great "I Am"? In what ways are you different because of that?

- How might Jesus be inviting you today to share the source of your joy with others?

- How has Jesus spoken to you in this devotional time?

## Prayer

Dear Jesus, thank you for your gift of joy. Please keep me close to you so that I can be truly be joy-full as I allow you to do your good work in me. Amen.

a spiritual practice
# CELEBRATING JUBILEE

As a way of reflecting on Jesus as "The Vine," and of celebrating all God has done in your life during the past few weeks, today you are invited to celebrate a modified version of an ancient biblical practice known as "Jubilee."

In the Old Testament, God commanded the Israelites to observe a year of Jubilee every fifty years. Jubilee involved forgiving debts, setting any indentured servants free and allowing the land to recover by lying fallow for a year. Any harvest that grew up on its own during Jubilee was available to everyone – rich and poor alike. In addition, all land was to revert back to its original owner during this year.

Jubilee was part of God's rhythm for His people, to keep them close to Him and caring for one another. God commanded His people to observe a Sabbath rest once every seven days (see Week 5 in this book for more explanation of Sabbath), and to observe a Sabbatical year once every seven years (when the land was allowed to rest), and to celebrate Jubilee after every seven cycles of Sabbaticals.

The purpose of Jubilee was to remind God's people that the earth belongs to the Lord, not to humans; it was a time of bringing God's justice to the poor and caring for the oppressed; it was a time of celebrating the truth that God is truly our Provider, not we ourselves; and Jubilee was a foreshadowing of God's future restoration of all creation, including true freedom for His children.

Ultimately, Jubilee is about living out God's greatest commandments to "Love the Lord your God with all your heart and with all your soul and with all your mind and with all your strength," and to, "Love your neighbor as yourself" (Mark 12:30-31). When we're living these principles, our priorities are straight; the things of this world lose their attraction; we are able to hold things more loosely; we are more generous toward others; and our character is more deeply changed to look like the character of Christ.

Today, declare your own personal Jubilee by reflecting on the following, then taking action. (*Note: You may decide to do today's exercises together with your small group or family. If so, see below.*)

## Idolatrous Attachments

Jesus said, "I am the vine, you are the branches… apart from me you can do nothing" (John 15:5). Although we may mentally understand what He's saying, we still struggle to live in true attachment to Jesus. Instead, we are more fundamentally attached to many other things: our possessions, status, goals, careers, family, identity, approval, success, leisure activities, image, emotional "highs", money, power, relationships, and the list could go on. These things are not bad in and of themselves, but anything we are attached to more than Jesus can become an idol in our lives, putting a wedge between us and God.

Spend some time with Jesus, asking Him to reveal the things you are most attached to in your life right now. Write them on a piece of paper. Ask for His help to surrender those attachments so that you can be more fully attached to Christ and filled with His true life.

## Detachment

Now ask Jesus to show you how to live with more detachment from the things of this world. When you're ready, symbolize your commitment to surrender your idolatrous attachments by crumpling up the paper and throwing it away – or even throwing it in the fireplace and burning it up.

You may also prayerfully consider giving away some of your material possessions to someone more in need of them. Ask God to show you whether He might call you to celebrate Jubilee by giving up some of your clothes, your food, your gardening tools, your technology, your money, your time, or something else. It might be most meaningful to give up something that represents the attachment you just surrendered. For example, if you find yourself overly attached to appearing good in the eyes of others, perhaps giving away some of your clothes or jewelry might help free you from that over-attachment.

Ask Jesus to give you a heart of joy in sharing the abundance of His good gifts with others. Pray for the needs of those you share with and ask God to bless them.

## Godly Attachment

After detaching yourself more from the things of this world, ask Jesus to help you become more attached to Him, the true Vine. You may want to close your time by celebrating the Lord's Supper (also called Communion or Eucharist). Before taking the bread and cup, read the following passages: Mark 14:22-24 and I Corinthians 11:23-26. As you take the elements, thank Jesus for surrendering His life so that you can have true life. As you are taking Him into yourself, remember that He is the Vine and you are the branch. Pray a prayer of commitment, telling Jesus of your desire to remain attached to Him.

## Celebrating with Your Family or Small Group

You may want to end your 50-day experience with Jesus, the great I AM, by celebrating "Jubilee" with your family or small group. Plan a time to meet together and walk through the steps in today's spiritual exercise. You may even want to have a follow-up time to collect items that your group wants to donate and then take them to a homeless shelter or some other charity.

If you decide to celebrate Communion together, you may want to consider serving each other at the table and praying for one another. It may also be meaningful to share with each other how Jesus has touched your life in the past 50 days.

# A LONG WALK with JESUS

Over the past fifty days, you have learned how Jesus' presence meets our deepest needs. Slowly and purposefully, Jesus has been revealing to you not only who He is, but the difference He makes. Jesus declares that He is the I AM, the God who is present and whose presence makes a difference. He is:

- the I AM, who offers us unconditional love.
- the Bread of Life, who fills and fulfills us.
- the Light of the World, who brings clarity and direction.
- the Good Shepherd, who makes us secure.
- the Resurrection and the Life, who give us a second chance and a new life.
- the Way, the Truth, and the Life, who tells the truth about the way to find life, purpose and God.
- the Vine, whose presence fills us with joy and enables us to be significant.

That is the difference Jesus makes as we nurture His presence in our lives.

Hopefully this book has helped you experience and nurture the presence of Jesus as you have done the daily Bible reading, prayer, and spiritual disciplines. We also hope you have been inspired by the people who have shared their personal stories. What Jesus has done for them, Jesus can also do for you.

Now, we urge you to continue this journey with Jesus for the rest of your life. With every step you take forward:

- Jesus grows in your life a little bit more.
- your needs are filled a little bit more.
- your faith grows stronger.

- temptations become weaker.
- your character becomes a little more godly.
- and the light of your life shines more radiantly.

Now, to close, let me tell you my story. It's a story of the difference Jesus makes over the long haul. I pray that it will inspire you to keep growing in your walk with Jesus.

## Phil Sommerville's Story

My story is about the blessings that come from walking closely with Jesus for a very long time. In my case, it's been generations.

For some, this story will be hard to relate to because it will be so different from the rough and tumble world you have experienced. But what I have found is that my experience is what most people hope they will experience someday. I am here to testify that the life you hope for is not just a wishful dream. It's real and can be experienced.

I hope my story will be an encouragement that you don't need to have a dramatic conversion in order to experience Jesus' presence. In fact, it may be Jesus' presence that has protected you from needing a dramatic conversion.

My parents were more than just church-goers. They had a relationship with Jesus that was obvious. They were products of Christian families. My grandparents also had an obvious love for Jesus. As a result, the blessings have cascaded down through the generations. In fact, there have been so many blessings, it's hard to know where to start.

Maybe the most obvious place to see the difference Jesus has made through the generations is in character. Galatians 5 describes godly character as the qualities of love, joy, peace, patience, kindness, goodness, gentleness, and self-control. Those qualities describe my grandparents' and my parents' lives. They had those qualities in abundance. The reason why, I believe, is because they had followed Jesus over a lifetime.

My grandparents did more than pop into church on Sundays. They lived God-honoring lives. They prayed daily and read their Bibles. In fact, my grandfather died, peacefully leaned back in his recliner, with his Bible across his chest. He had been studying his Sunday school lesson.

Jesus shined through my grandparents' lives. There was no quick temper, no heated arguments, no cussing and cursing, no lying or deceit, no overt selfish behavior, and no self-destructive behaviors.

My grandparents were godly people. So not surprisingly, their marriages were blessed as well. My grandparents really loved each other, and it showed in the way they treated each other. They honored each other, served each other, supported each other, affirmed each other, treasured each other, playfully teased each other, and disagreed with each other, but worked it out quickly. In short, they really loved each other.

These are the homes my parents grew up in, and it made a difference in their lives. My parents developed their own, vibrant faith in Jesus, which they nourished daily. They prayed and studied their Bibles, had Christian fellowship and support, and found ways to serve – from teaching Sunday school to sewing quilts for others.

My parent's character exuded the fruit of the Spirit. I experienced unconditional love, joy, peace (I never realized how peaceful my home was until I grew up and heard war stories from others), plenty of patience, kindness, goodness, and everything else, and not just towards me but towards others as well.

Like their parents before them, my parent's marriage was rock-solid and loving. Even in their disagreements, or maybe especially in their disagreements, they showed love and kindness towards each other. They were always building each other up.

Because my parents and grandparents lived God-honoring lives, they made God-honoring choices that kept them and their families out of trouble. Because they didn't do things that would be harmful, they were protected from the pain of poor decisions. Some cynical people might call their life safe and boring. I know differently. I call it blessed.

So that's the environment I grew up in. Looking back, I guess you could call it an idyllic home life, but to me it was just normal. I grew up in a protective cocoon of love that had been built up over generations of walking closely with Jesus. I am the recipient of blessings that have cascaded down from the godly lives of my parents and grandparents.

In some ways, I've been walking with Jesus since the day I was born. But there have been commitment points along the way where I've made that walk personal and have experienced Jesus' presence for myself. When I was seven, I walked down the aisle of my church to personally accept Jesus as my Savior. When I was a high school senior, I started to experience the reality of Jesus' presence in my own life. After I graduated, I sensed a calling from God to go into ministry as my profession. But those points, as well as others that followed, were just what you might call an extra nudge of awareness of Jesus' presence.

Through a lifetime of walking with Jesus, my own character is being developed and strengthened. My continuous prayer is that my perceptions, attitudes, thoughts, actions and reactions will increasingly be those of Jesus. It is my desire that as people get to know me, they will get at least a glimpse of the real and living Jesus who is in me.

It is His presence that shapes and fills me, protects me and my family, and guides my decisions. Because of His presence I am blessed with:

- a marriage that keeps getting better.
- a home that reminds me daily of God's goodness.
- a peace and joy that defies my circumstances.
- a love that I know is special, but has always just been normal to me.
- a hope that comes from being certain God is with me.
- a purpose to help others experience how real God is.
- a sense of fullness that I struggle to explain (the best description I've been able to think of is that it is the weight of God's presence serving as a ballast in my life).
- and a legacy that I am passing on to my sons.

That's the difference Jesus, the I AM, makes in a life. It's a blessed life and I can testify that it's real because it is my story – or more accurately, it is the story of Jesus in my life. My prayer is that this will be your story as well and that this book has helped you on that journey.

# A Prayer of Salvation

## Beginning Your Journey with Jesus

If you're ready to begin a relationship with Jesus Christ, simply tell Him. He's waiting for you. Feel free to use the prayer below, or simply speak from your heart.

Dear Jesus,

I need you in my life. I know I can't earn your approval, and I can't find the joy and peace I need apart from you. Thank you for your death on the cross and your resurrection from the dead – all so that I could be free from sin and have a relationship with God. Please come into my life and forgive me for my sin. Help me to follow you and allow you to change me from the inside-out. Give me a new heart and new life in you. I am yours. Amen.

# The Seven I AMs of Jesus

## Small Group Bible Studies

# Study 1 "I Am He"

## OPENING

1. If this is a new group, spend some time introducing yourselves.

2. Which of Jesus' "I am" statements appeals to you the most? Explain why. (Skip this question if introductions went long)

I am He

I am the Bread of Life

I am the Light of the World

I am the Good Shepherd

I am the Resurrection and the Life

I am the Way, the Truth and the Life

I am the Vine

## BIBLE STUDY

1. Read John 4:1-42. Share what stands out to you from this encounter.

### BACKGROUND

The antipathy between Jews and Samaritans went back centuries. When the kingdoms of Israel and Judah were conquered, nearly all Jews were forcibly relocated to other lands. The Samaritans were the descendants of the few Jews who were not relocated. Over time, they intermarried outside the Jewish faith – a violation of God's law. When the Jews returned, the Samaritans tried to reunite with their brethren but were rejected. The two groups despised each other ever since. In Jesus' day, Jews would choose to spend an extra day to travel around Samaria rather than go through Samaria. On top of that, Jewish rabbis tried never to speak to a woman in public. So, imagine this Samaritan woman's double surprise when Jesus spoke to her.

2. Do you think this woman was thirsty for something more in life? Why or why not?

3. What about you, what is your deepest thirst?

4. When Jesus spoke to the woman about "living water" what did she picture? What kind of water was Jesus talking about? What does that suggest about the kind of thirst Jesus thinks is the greater concern?

# Study 1 "I Am He"

5. Why would Jesus ask the woman to go and get her husband when He clearly knew that she was not married?

6. In verse 17, the woman told the truth, but did so in a way that tried to hide the truth. We often do the same thing. Why do you think she was hiding the truth? Why do we try to hide some truths?

7. In verses 17-18, Jesus reveals that He knew the whole truth about the woman, but there was something else that the woman was probably expecting from Jesus that didn't happen. If you were a Samaritan woman and you just had your secret exposed, what would you have expected from a Jewish rabbi? What did she experience instead? How did this touch her deepest thirst?

8. When Jesus told the Samaritan woman, "I am He," in verse 26, what was He saying? How can you tell if the woman understood?

9. Looking at this story, how would you identify the steps this woman took towards faith in Jesus?

10. How are these steps the same or different from the steps you took, or are taking, towards faith in Jesus?

## MAKING IT PERSONAL

1. Does the image of Jesus being present in your life as a spring of living water appeal to you? Why or why not?

2. What did Jesus say the woman needed to do to receive this living water? Does this surprise you? Why?

3. Reread verse 42. Why is this an important statement? What causes you to believe in Jesus?

4. If we believe in Jesus, His living water is present in our lives. But we don't always take a drink. Do you have a story you can share of a time when you stopped drinking from the living water? What happened?

5. When do you drink from Jesus' living water? How often will you do it?

## PRAYER

Think about where you are thirsty in your life right now. Do you believe Jesus can quench that thirst? Say a prayer asking for His living water.

# Study 2  "I Am the Bread of Life"

## OPENING

1.  Do you think people have a need to feel fulfilled? Explain.

## BIBLE STUDY

1.  The day after He fed 5,000 people with only five loaves of bread and two fish (John 6:1-15), Jesus announced that He was "the bread of life." Many of the people He spoke to had either witnessed or heard about that miracle. Read John 6:25-51. What are the people looking for and what is Jesus offering? What is the difference?

### BACKGROUND

Manna is the bread God provided the Israelites during the forty years they spent in the wilderness before entering the Promised Land. Manna represents God's provision for His people (you can read about it in Exodus 16). In Jesus' day, the rabbis had been teaching that the Messiah would again provide manna. This is likely why the crowd was asking Jesus for manna, despite having just witnessed the feeding of the 5,000. Jesus uses this request to teach them about the kind of Messiah He really is and to tell them that what He has to offer has value far beyond mere bread.

2.  In what ways does Jesus compare Himself to manna? What does Jesus say is the difference(s) between Himself, as the Bread of Life, and manna? What is the point Jesus is trying to make by these comparisons?

3.  Why do you think the people are having such a hard time understanding what Jesus is teaching them?

4.  How would you summarize the lessons to be learned from this passage? How is it relevant today? Why do you need the Bread of Life?

## MAKING IT PERSONAL

1.  What kinds of "junk food," spiritual or material, do people seek in an effort to find fulfillment?

# Study 2 "I Am the Bread of Life"

2.  Read the following passages. How is a life spent in pursuit of material things described in each of these passages? What do they all have in common?

    Job 20:4-5
    Hebrews 11:25
    Matthew 6:19-21
    1 Timothy 6:8-10, 17
    1 John 2:16-17
    Ephesians 2:1-3

3.  Now read the following verses about the life Jesus wants to fill you with.

    Galatians 5:22-23
    Ephesians 3:14-19
    Romans 6:21-23
    Romans 15:13
    2 Timothy 1:7

    What are the differences between this life and the one described in question two?

4.  In John 6:52-59, Jesus explains how we can experience the presence of the Bread of Life. Read the passage and then consider the following questions:    What does Jesus mean when He tells us to eat His flesh and drink His blood? Have you ever heard people say, "I need to chew on that"? How about, "I could eat you up"? How can those phrases help you understand what Jesus is teaching? How do we practice this teaching so that we can experience the blessings of the Bread of Life?

5.  Consider the descriptions of life found in questions #2 and #3 above. How does your own life match up with those descriptions? Share with the group a characteristic you want to see less of in your life and a characteristic you want to strengthen.

## PRAYER

Take time to pray for each other regarding the changes you want to make in your life.

# Study 3 "I Am the Light of the World"

## OPENING

1. Divide into two teams and as a team brainstorm as many answers as you can think of for these questions: What does light do? What are its benefits? The team with the longest list is the winner. The group leader will be the judge on whether an item on your list is legitimate and his/her ruling cannot be disputed.

## BIBLE STUDY

1. To understand the background of Jesus' dramatic statement, "I am the light of the world," read the introduction to week 3 on page 73. Given the lamp lighting ceremony as a background to this statement, what would the crowds have understood Jesus to be claiming?

2. Read John 8:12-30. From Jesus' declaration and the debate that followed, what can you learn about what Jesus is referring to by His use of the terms "light" and "dark"?

3. Read John 8:31. What does knowing the truth have to do with light?

4. Read John 8:32-47. From this conversation, what else (if anything) do you learn about what truth, light and darkness mean? What does the truth set you free from? How does the truth set you free?

5. Read Matthew 8:11-12. Given how Jesus uses the word "darkness" in these verses, why is light so important?

6. Read John 3:19-21. According to these verses, what is the function of Jesus' light? Why is it so important? Is this a good or bad thing?

7. Read Matthew 5:14-16. What happens when the light of Jesus fills our life?

8. From what you've learned, what does Jesus' declaration that "I am the light of the world" tell you about what His presence can do in your life?

## MAKING IT PERSONAL

1. In what ways have you experienced the kind of darkness in your life that Jesus has been talking about?

2. In what area of your life do you need to experience the light of Jesus? Where do you need Him to shine?

# Study 3 "I Am the Light of the World"

3. Read John 1:4-13. We need Jesus, the "Light of the World," because without Him our hearts would be dark. According to these verses, what is the first step we must take to experience the light of Jesus? (If you have never taken this step you are encouraged to use the prayer of salvation on page 219 to receive Jesus Christ as your Savior.)

4. Read Ephesians 5:8-14. Once we have received the "Light of the World" what steps are we taught to take and why?

5. Read Psalm 119:105. We need the "Light of the World" because we confront darkness every day. According to Psalm 119:105, what tool must you use if you want to be guided by Jesus' light? How does this relate to John 3:19-21, the passage you read in question #6, and the Ephesians 5:8-14 passage you just read?

6. Read 1 John 1:5-9. How does confession relate to walking in the light? How does it relate to truth and being set free?

## PRAYER

Confession is an invaluable tool that allows Jesus' light to transform our lives. Through Bible study, Christian friends and personal reflection, Jesus' light will reveal sins in your life. Through confession, you unleash the power of Jesus to cleanse you of those sins.

Confession is an act of prayer where you admit the truth so that you can be set free. It will sound something like this:

*"Dear Jesus, I did _____. I renounce it as wrong, I make no excuse for it, and I choose to turn away from that sin to walk into your light and follow your ways. Amen"*

When you sin, you commit specific acts. So make sure your confession is also as specific as possible.

Take a few minutes of silence now for a time of silent confession. First ask Jesus to shine His light into your heart and reveal to you any sins that need to be confessed. Perhaps, if there is time, you can use the Prayer of Examen exercise from Day 21. As things come to mind (and they will), use the prayer above to confess those sins and experience the blessings of the "Light of the World."

# Study 4 "I Am the Good Shepherd"

## OPENING

1. Finish the following sentence: The thing that makes me most anxious is....

## BIBLE STUDY

1. Read John 10:1-10. What dangers do the sheep face? How have you experienced any of these threats in a real or figurative way in your own life?

2. Before identifying Himself as the Good Shepherd, Jesus first says, "I am the gate." In this passage, what function does the gate have? What is Jesus saying about Himself and the difference He makes?

3. Read John 10:11-18. What makes Jesus the "Good" Shepherd?

4. Jesus says that the shepherd owns his sheep. In what way does Jesus, the Good Shepherd, "own" you?

5. What can you count on because you are owned by Jesus?

6. Read John 10:22-33. What does it mean that "no one can snatch (you) out of the Father's hand?" What difference can trusting that truth make when:

   - You make a bad mistake?
   - Feel tempted?
   - Feel anxious or worried?

7. Read Joshua 1:9, Psalm 23:4, and 1 John 4:4. What is the common theme in these verses that can help you feel secure?

8. Read John 10:10 again. From everything you have learned so far from this series, how would you describe the "life to the full" that Jesus offers?

## MAKING IT PERSONAL

1. How do sheep learn to recognize and follow the voice of their shepherd?

2. Share specific ideas on how we can learn to be more aware of Jesus' presence and recognize and follow His voice.

# Study 4 "I Am the Good Shepherd"

3.  What is the next step you need to take to more fully experience the Good Shepherd in your life?

## PRAYER

Together, read the following verses aloud.

*"Cast all your anxiety on him because he cares for you." 1 Peter 5:7*

*"Do not be anxious about anything, but in every situation, by prayer and petition, with thanksgiving, present your requests to God. And the peace of God, which transcends all understanding, will guard your hearts and your minds in Christ Jesus." Philippians 4:6-7*

Use your prayer time to practice these verses.

1.  If you have an anxiety, please share it, but no more than one anxiety per person.

2.  Perhaps have each person pray for the person on their left.

3.  When you pray, you will want to focus first on God, not the anxiety. Think of an attribute of God that would be the answer to the anxiety. For example, if the anxiety relates to finances, the attribute of God could be Provider.

4.  Launch your prayer time by praising God for the attribute you chose, and then pray briefly for the anxiety that was shared by the person you are praying for.

5.  When everybody has had a chance to pray like this, move into a time where anyone can offer a prayer of thanks for ways they have seen God work in their life. According to Philippians 4, when you pray with thanksgiving, the peace of God will guard your heart and mind from the grip of fear and anxiety.

# Study 5 "I Am the Resurrection and the Life"

## OPENING

1. Finish the following sentence: One way Jesus has changed my life is...

## BIBLE STUDY

1. Read John 11:1-44. Pay attention to the person or group in this story that comes closest to representing how you are feeling in your life right now. Share your answer with the group.

2. Why do you think Jesus delayed His arrival?

3. How would you describe Martha and Mary's faith in Jesus? Given the circumstances, does that surprise you? Explain.

4. Jesus makes a point of asking Martha, "Do you believe this?" What do you think Jesus is looking for when He asks this? Why does He push the issue?

5. When Jesus says "I am the resurrection and the life," what is He revealing about Himself? Do you think Martha really understood? Explain.

6. Read the following statement:

   Martha almost prevents the resurrection of Lazarus. She rightly points out that it will stink if the tomb gets opened. Before you can experience a resurrection in any area of your life, you have to "open the tomb." But sometimes we prevent a resurrection from happening in our lives because we are afraid to open up our lives and reveal the "stink" within.

   What's your reaction? Do you agree or disagree with this statement? Why?

## MAKING IT PERSONAL

1. What "deaths" (physical, spiritual, emotional, relational, etc.) are you facing in your life? Are you struggling with something (or someone) in your life that seems almost beyond hope? If you're able, consider sharing this with the group.

# Study 5 "I Am the Resurrection and the Life"

2. It appears that everyone in the story had a limit to what they believed Jesus could do. But then they experienced for themselves what it meant to be in the presence of the "Resurrection and the Life." In what ways have you had, or do you have, a limit to what you believe Jesus can do?

3. "Do you believe this?" If you really believe that Jesus *is* the Resurrection and the Life, what difference would it make in the way you:

   - deal with your problems?
   - view others?
   - view your future?

4. Is there a story you can share about a way you have experienced a personal resurrection?

## PRAYER

Break up into pairs or trios, men with men and women with women. In these smaller groups, share a place in your life where you want to experience a resurrection. Then, pray and ask Jesus to bring his resurrection power into each other's lives in those areas. Make a pact to continue praying for each other and to let each other know when Jesus answers.

# Study 6  "I Am the Way, the Truth, and the Life"

## OPENING

1.  Describe a time when you were really lost (literally, not figuratively).

## BIBLE STUDY

1.  In any endeavor in life, what happens if you don't commit to a way?

2.  Read John 14:1-11.  Why would people consider Jesus' declaration in verse 6 arrogant? What evidence can you think of that would prove that Jesus was not being arrogant?

3.  According to this passage, what is Jesus "the way" to?

4.  What else is Jesus the way to? Divide the following passages up among the group to be read out loud. After each is read, decide as a group on a word or couple of words that describe what that passage says Jesus is the way to.

    - John 10:10
    - John 8:32
    - John 11:25
    - Ephesians 2:10
    - Philippians 4:13
    - Galatians 5:22-23
    - John 10:28

5.  What do you think Jesus means when he declares that He is *the* truth?

6.  What difference would knowing the truth make…

    - in listening to a sales pitch?
    - in choosing a spouse?
    - in serving on a jury?
    - in living your life?

7.  What difference would knowing the truth about yourself make?

8.  Why do we sometimes not want to know the truth about ourselves?

9.  Jesus declares Himself to be *the* life. Maybe the best way to learn about the life Jesus offers is to look at what happened to the people in the following stories. If you're not familiar with the story, or need a refresher, look up the passage. What do you learn about the life Jesus

# Study 6 "I Am the Way, the Truth, and the Life"

offers from each event?

- The woman at the well (John 4:1-42)
- Lazarus rising from the dead (John 11:1-44)
- Peter walking on the water (Matthew 14:22-32)
- Paul, the worst of sinners (1 Timothy 1:12-17)
- Paul in the Philippian prison (Acts 16:22-34)

## MAKING IT PERSONAL

1. If Jesus is the true way to life, then what does that mean about the way we need to live?

2. What difference would it make in your life, knowing that you're on the way to heaven?

3. How does the following quote affirm or add to your understanding about the difference Jesus "*the Way*" makes.

   *"Our assurance of heaven ought to be a powerful motivation each day of our lives... The allurement of temptation and the burdens of pain and sorrow are diminished and often removed when we let the expectation of heaven take over in our minds and hearts." Warren Wiersbe*

4. Do you know the way of salvation? If you don't, keep reading.

## EXPLAINING WHY JESUS IS THE ONLY WAY TO GOD

1. You are a sinner. *"For all sin and fall short of God's glory"* (Romans 3:23).

2. Sin is a problem. *"The wages of sin is death"* (Romans 6:23).

3. Jesus' death is the only thing that pays the penalty for sin. *"But God demonstrates his own love for us in this: While we were still sinners, Christ died for us"* (Romans 5:8).

4. Jesus rose from the dead, giving us hope and new life. *"In his great mercy he has given us new birth into a living hope through the resurrection of Jesus Christ from the dead"* (1 Peter 1:3).

# Study 6 "I Am the Way, the Truth, and the Life"

5. Because of Jesus' actions we can:
   - Be forgiven. *"I am writing to you, dear children, because your sins have been forgiven on account of his name"* (1 John 2:12).
   - Have a close relationship with God. *"See what great love the Father has lavished on us, that we should be called children of God!"* (1 John 3:1)
   - Have eternal life. *"I give them eternal life, and they shall never perish"* (John 10:28).

6. To receive this gift of salvation we must:
   - Believe in Jesus. *"Whoever believes in the Son has eternal life"* (John 3:36)
   - Follow Jesus. *"We know that we have come to know him if we keep his commands"* (1 John 2:3).

7. Are you ready to invite Jesus into your life? If so, turn to the prayer of salvation on page 219.

8. Tell your group (or at least your group leader) if you prayed that prayer!

## PRAYER

To allow Jesus to fill you with life, you need to commit yourself to His way. In prayer, make a commitment to be a sold-out follower of Jesus Christ. Tell Jesus you are making a commitment to obeying Him completely. Ask Him to give you the strength to obey and the awareness of where you are going off track. If you are serious about your commitment, why not let everyone know by boldly praying this prayer out loud?

# Study 7 "I Am the True Vine"

## OPENING

1. What kind of a legacy would you like to leave after you die?

## BIBLE STUDY

1. Read John 15:1-13, then fill in the blanks below.

   When we _____, we obey Christ's command. (vs. 12)

   When we obey Christ's command, we _____. (vs. 10)

   When we remain in Jesus' love, we will _____. (vs. 5)

   When we are fruitful, we will experience _____. (vs. 11)

2. Looking back at question #1, what is the recipe for experiencing joy?

3. When you hear the word "obey," what is the first thought that comes to your mind?

4. Some people think obedience is contradictory to God's grace and to freedom in Christ. What do you think? How does obedience relate to fruitfulness, grace and freedom? Consider the following questions as you form your answer.

   *When playing a sport, are there rules and best practices that will help you succeed if you follow them?*

   *At work, are there policies and procedures that will help you succeed if you obey them?*

   *When flying in an airplane, are there laws and procedures that must be obeyed in order to ensure safety?*

5. Why does Jesus single out the command to love others as He has loved us, saying that this is the most important way we are to obey Him?

6. Does being "fruitful" (and we're not talking about child-bearing) sound like something you would want to be known for? Explain.

7. Given what Jesus says in verses 9-13 about what it means to remain in His love, what do you think it means to be fruitful?

## MAKING IT PERSONAL

1. After studying this passage, what did you learn about the difference the presence of Jesus, "the true vine," will make in your life?

# Study 7 "I Am the True Vine"

2. A vinedresser prunes back a branch so that the life-giving sap of the vine can be used to produce fruit instead of making excess leaves. What kind of excess baggage in your life (good or bad) might be limiting your fruitfulness? What will you do about it?

3. When Jesus tells the disciples to remain in Him, He is revealing that it's also possible to disconnect from Him. So, even though the presence of Jesus is in us, that doesn't mean we are drawing from the life of "The Vine." We must intentionally remain connected.

   There are many ways to remain in Jesus, but in this passage Jesus is teaching a very specific way – obedience to loving others as He has loved us. When we do that, others will enjoy the fruit, and we will experience complete joy.

   What is the next step you want to take in order to more fully obey this command of Jesus?

4. SUGGESTION: Set a date to have a party to celebrate the completion of this series. Have everyone bring their favorite dessert or snack. During the celebration, share stories about the lessons you have learned and the ways you have grown and experienced the presence of Jesus. Be sure to share these stories with your pastor(s). Also, please share them with us at www.theSevenIAmsofJesus.com

## SHARE YOUR STORY

Over these last fifty days you have read 43 stories of people like yourself who have experienced the difference Jesus, the I AM, has made in their lives. You also have a story to share, and God can use it to inspire and bless others. Please, share your story at **www.theSevenIAmsofJesus.com** and while you're there be blessed by the stories of others.

## PRAYER

Share prayer requests and then pray, following the pattern below.

1. Choose the "I am" that has been the most meaningful to you and praise God for being that "I am."

2. Thank God for what you have seen Him do these past seven weeks.

3. Pray for your requests.

# About the Authors

Phil and Linda Sommerville are the founders of Faith Alive 365, a ministry that provides creative resources to help people come more fully alive in Christ every day, not just on Sundays.

Their love for God and His people have led them to serve in a wide range of ministries during their lives, including experience as church planters, small groups pastor, Christian University faculty, mission workers, worship leader, para-church ministry, retreat speaking, and writing. With a blend of openness and wit, they love sharing the lessons they have learned about developing a thriving relationship with Christ and are frequent speakers at churches and retreats.

Phil and Linda have been married for more than twenty years and have two terrific teenage sons. Together they enjoy camping in the redwoods, making homemade ice cream, playing Dutch Blitz, watching a good murder mystery, and continuing to learn how to speak techno-jargon with their sons.

# Ever wonder if you're missing something?

Like maybe there's some secret to living a fulfilling Christian life, but you haven't been let in on it? If so, you're not alone. Many people just like you wonder if they will ever be able to move beyond surviving to thriving. Faith Alive 365 is committed to helping people experience real, God-sized living — 365 days a year!

# Small Group Bible Studies

**Living a God-Sized Life**

**Fired Up**
Book of Acts

**Money Matters**
How God Uses Money as a Tool
for Building Faith

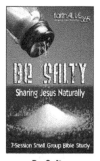

**Be Salty**
Sharing Your Faith
Naturally

**Start Strong**
4 week Study for New
Believers

**Power Up**
4 week Study for New
Believers

**Break Free**
4 week Study for New
Believers

## www.FaithAlive365.com

## 40 DAYS WITH THE SHEPHERD

### A FRESH LOOK AT PSALM 23

In this 40-day devotional book, Psalm 23 will come alive in fresh new ways. Learn directly from David how you can experience God as powerfully as David experienced God.

# Also available as an All-Church Series
## Have your entire church learn and grow together!

Church kit includes:
- A copy of the *StressBusters* daily devotional Book
- 7 Sermons with slides and bulletin outlines
- Reproducible small group studies with Leader's Guides
- Artwork
- Instructions on running this series at your church

## www.FaithAlive365.com

Share *The Seven I AMs of Jesus* with your entire church!

# The Seven I AMs of Jesus
# All-Church Series

*The Seven I AMs* all-church series combines this book with a 7-week sermon series so that your entire congregation can be focused together on experiencing the powerful presence of Jesus. Through the weekly worship, daily devotions and weekly small group studies, God can move powerfully in your church.

### *The Seven I AMs* All-Church Series Kit includes:

- A copy of this Daily Devotional Book
- 7 Sermons with slides and bulletin outlines
- Leader Guides for the Small Group Studies
- Artwork
- Instructions on running this series at your church

*"We had some really amazing things happen during the series. People came to faith who we'd been working with for quite some time. Record numbers joined small groups. People LOVED the book. We had long time believers reenergized in their faith. We had our largest community service event ever. HUGE thanks to you for this excellent series."*

Randy Sherwood, Pastor of Bayside Church of Plumas Lake, CA

## Order from www.FaithAlive365.com